SUGIHARA CHIUNE

JAPAN LIBRARY

SUGIHARA CHIUNE

The Duty and Humanity
of an Intelligence Officer

SHIRAISHI Masaaki

Translated by Gaynor Sekimori

Japan Publishing Industry Foundation for Culture

Note to the reader:
This book follows the Hepburn system of romanization for Japanese words and the Pinyin system for Chinese words. For proper nouns and terms with official romanizations, the official romanizations are used even if they do not follow these styles. Except for citations and references to works that were published with macrons, the use of macrons has been omitted from the text. Long vowels in reference citations are rendered as single letters rather than double letters, except for "ei." The tradition of placing the family name first has been followed for Japanese and Chinese names. The official titles used in this book are the official English translations used by the relevant Japanese authorities. For this English edition, the chronological table and reference list have been revised for the reader, and a list of notable persons has been added to the text.

Sugihara Chiune: The Duty and Humanity of an Intelligence Officer
Shiraishi Masaaki. Translated by Gaynor Sekimori.

Published by
Japan Publishing Industry Foundation for Culture (JPIC)
2-2-30 Kanda-Jinbocho, Chiyoda-ku, Tokyo 101-0051, Japan

First English edition: March 2021

This book is a translation of *Sugihara Chiune: Jōhō ni kaketa gaikōkan* published by SHINCHOSHA Publishing Co., Ltd. in paperback format in 2015. Its original edition was published by the same publisher in 2011 under the title of *Chōhō no tensai Sugihara Chiune*.
English publishing rights arranged with SHINCHOSHA Publishing Co., Ltd., Tokyo.

Book design: Miki Kazuhiko, Ampersand Works

Printed in Japan
ISBN 978-4-86658-174-3
https://japanlibrary.jpic.or.jp/

CONTENTS

Maps

Europe

-------- Polish border, interwar period
⨯⨯⨯⨯⨯⨯⨯⨯⨯⨯ East Prussia (now Russian territory), interwar period

Northeast China at the time of the Manchurian Incident

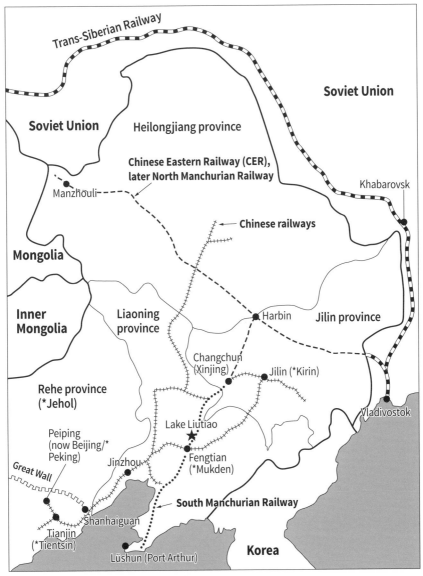

Trans-Siberian Railway

Soviet Union

Soviet Union

Heilongjiang province

Chinese Eastern Railway (CER), later North Manchurian Railway

Khabarovsk

Manzhouli

Chinese railways

Mongolia

Inner Mongolia

Liaoning province

Harbin

Jilin province

Changchun (Xinjing)

Jilin (*Kirin)

Rehe province (*Jehol)

Lake Liutiao

Vladivostok

Peiping (now Beijing/* Peking)

Great Wall

Jinzhou

Fengtian (*Mukden)

South Manchurian Railway

Shanhaiguan

Tianjin (*Tientsin)

Lüshun (Port Arthur)

Korea

* widely used transcription/usage in the 1930s

AUTHOR'S INTRODUCTION TO THE ENGLISH EDITION

I am delighted that people all over the world will be able to read my study of Sugihara Chiune through this English translation.

This book is a revised and expanded version of my 2011 work *Chōhō no tensai Sugihara Chiune* (Sugihara Chiune, genius of intelligence).

Sugihara Chiune, a Japanese diplomat, is celebrated for saving the lives of several thousand Jewish refugees attempting to escape from Soviet and German threats during the Second World War by issuing them Japanese transit visas. In the original 2011 edition, I depicted the life of Sugihara as a diplomat and how he issued the "visas for life," referring in the main to records preserved in the Diplomatic Archives of the Japanese Ministry of Foreign Affairs. The result was that, whereas former studies had described him as a great humanitarian, I showed him to be an outstanding intelligence officer as well as a humanitarian. Happily, many of my Japanese readers acknowledged that my book had provided further insight into important aspects of Sugihara's personality, and I was honored that it was used as a reference for the first film to be made about the man, Cellin Gluck's *Persona Non Grata* (2015).

The production of the film gave me a rare opportunity to publish an expanded and revised edition of *Chōhō no tensai Sugihara Chiune*. This new edition incorporates the results of research carried out since the earlier publication. I focused in particular on what I believe to be the most important aspect of research into Sugihara: the ingenuity he showed in issuing the visas. I am proud to have been able to elaborate on this aspect more than I could in the previous edition of this book. And while it is well known that Sugihara issued visas in Kaunas in Lithuania, he did the same during his next posting in Prague (in what was then Czechoslovakia) as well. This was mentioned briefly in the previous edition, but I devoted a full chapter to the subject in this edition.

It is the greatest good fortune that this new edition has now been translated into English. I would like to express my deepest gratitude to the many people who have helped to bring this about.

At a time when the issue of refugees has become critical in many parts of the world, I sincerely hope that this book will serve as a catalyst that prompts as many people as possible to take a personal interest in the plight of refugees.

The Good Listener

"Those are stamps! Most of the text is stamps!" I involuntarily let out a cry as I drank in the image of the visa on my screen. During the Second World War, the diplomat Sugihara Chiune saved many lives by issuing large numbers of Japanese transit visas to Jewish refugees who had found themselves caught in perilous circumstances in Europe. I have been researching him for more than thirty years, but I will never forget the bolt from the blue I experienced at that moment.

The most important evidence for Sugihara research is the visas themselves, but the people who possessed them would not readily give them up, and so it was very difficult to study those originals in detail. And there was no reason why they should not wish to hold on to them. After all, these visas had saved their lives, enabling them to escape from war-torn Europe. These treasured pieces of paper they had kept safe were too important to donate, even if they could contribute to advancing research.

However, digital imagery, email, and other advances in technology have changed the situation completely. Even if people do not want to make the originals available, more and more are making digital images accessible for research. I am delighted to have been able to access a number of them. By checking them in detail and comparing them, I have often come across new facts. But it was my encounter with the visa stamp I mentioned above that brought me face to face with a completely unexpected fact.

I had thought that Sugihara's issuance of such a large number of visas in a very short time, with him writing out the required information by hand, would have required almost superhuman effort. However, in the case of the visa shown on my screen, what astounded me was that almost all the text, including Sugihara's signature, was stamped. This discovery, which was only made possible because the digital image enabled even the slightest variations in the ink to be seen, gave me fresh insight into Sugihara's persona, and made me realize once again that there were still unexplored depths in the study of Sugihara Chiune (see Chapter Six).

My research on Sugihara began in 1990 when I read a book called *Rokusennin no inochi no biza* (Visas for life for six thousand) by his wife, Sugihara Yukiko. By coincidence, that year marked exactly fifty years since Sugihara had saved large numbers of people by issuing Japanese transit visas to Jewish and other refugees in Kaunas, Lithuania. He was little known at that time, but now, I am pleased to say, he has attracted the interest of people throughout the world.

I have been privileged to make many contacts in the course of my incessant study of Sugihara, and my research continues today. I feel inexpressible joy when I unexpectedly come across important information, such as the visa above, that helps to lift the veil of mystery that enshrouds the figure of Sugihara Chiune, even if only by a tiny amount.

I am very fortunate in terms of my research that I work at the Diplomatic Archives of the Ministry of Foreign Affairs. Its archive is classified and filed according to subject matter, and there is no single file where all the records connected with Sugihara are kept. I think about incidents and subject matter that might be connected to Sugihara, make a guess about how they could be classified, and then search file by file. This requires a lot of perseverance, and I am overjoyed when my efforts are rewarded with the discovery of a relevant document. It is like a treasure hunt. Though it may seem unspectacular work from the outside, for a researcher, it is a truly thrilling and enjoyable occupation.

During the time I was bringing the results of my research together piece by piece in academic articles, I was blessed by an unexpected turn of events. Professor Teshima Ryūichi of the Graduate School at Keio University visited me at the Diplomatic Archives and invited me to take up the challenge of depicting the persona of Sugihara Chiune in a new way. This did not mean damaging his existing image as a humanitarian, but rather describing him from another angle, that of an intelligence officer. It seemed to me that the best approach might be to sift attentively through the materials at my disposal and allow Sugihara to speak to me from between the lines. If this proved possible, I was ready to take up the challenge. This book is the result of my decision to do so.

"Intelligence activities" refers to the gathering of valuable information and sifting through it carefully to make it useful for the future. The word *interi-jensu* ("intelligence") is finally beginning to be understood in Japan, but it may not yet be generally recognized. The Japanese word *chōhō* ("espionage") is widely used also as a gloss for "intelligence," putting a somewhat negative slant on intelligence activities. Readers of this book, however, will appreciate that Sugihara saved a great many lives through his intelligence activities and had access to critical information that could possibly have averted the war if its recipients had used it appropriately. And if that war could only have been prevented, heaven knows how much tragedy could have been avoided.

Sugihara's intelligence work never led to war or disorder. On the contrary, it was undertaken to bring peace and order to people. This is why I have focused on Sugihara Chiune as an intelligence officer.

Of course, I do not in the least deny that Sugihara was a great human-itarian. He saved several thousand lives just in Kaunas, and it is said that today 250,000 people owe their lives to him, if we include the children, grandchildren, and great-grandchildren of the survivors. And as this book shows, he also saved a large number of people in Prague, and if we ever find out exactly what happened there, still more lives may be added to the list of those saved through his actions.

In 1985, Israel honored Sugihara as one of the Righteous Among the Nations. This is an honorific bestowed on non-Jews who, at the risk of their own lives, saved the lives of Jews during the Holocaust. Sugihara is the only Japanese to have received this honor so far. Inscribed on the medal awarded to recipients are the words (in Hebrew) "Whoever saves a single life, saves an entire universe." Sugihara did everything he could to save each and every refugee who came knocking at his door. He probably never imagined the number would reach several thousand. But the visas he issued in the fervent hope that they would save lives are indeed linked to the lives of many more than this number.

As a result, there is no doubt that Sugihara Chiune continues to make a strong impression on a great many people, but it would be a shame if he were known only for his humanitarian side. The time has come for a deeper study of the man.

The possibility of conducting interviews with relevant people is one of the most attractive aspects of conducting research on contemporary history. In this sense, it was indeed fortunate that research on Sugihara began at a time when there were still a large number of people living who had known him, enabling many interviews to be conducted. These interviews constitute an oral history that makes up the bulk of the first stage of research into Sugihara, when the expression "Sugihara the Humanitarian" was immortalized. Today, however, many people associated with Sugihara have died, including his wife Yukiko (on October 8, 2008), and there is little likelihood that any new facts will emerge from interviews now.

A new, second stage of research now seems to be needed. The novel *Sugihara darā* (Sugihara dollar) by Teshima Ryūichi has pointed in this direction, shedding light as it does on Sugihara Chiune as an intelligence officer. In his book *1991 nen Nihon no haiboku* (1991, the year of Japan's defeat), Teshima compared an excellent intelligence officer to a hare with long ears. This is an apt metaphor. The ability to cast a wide net to gather information in the field is fundamental to intelligence. In other words, an intelligence officer needs the long ears of a hare, and like a hare, needs to be shrewd but not aggressive. As will become clear in this book, intelligence activities require unimaginably long and steadfast perseverance.

Former refugees had no way of knowing about Sugihara's activities as an intelligence officer, since by definition those activities were carried out in secrecy. He did not speak of his work in any detail, even to his wife, Yukiko, the person closest to him. As this book reveals, during his time working at the consulate-general in Königsberg (present-day Kaliningrad) he achieved great success as an intelligence officer, but Mrs. Sugihara made no reference at all to this in her memoir.

In pursuing this aspect of Sugihara's life, it was necessary to examine the documentary evidence meticulously, based on revelations uncovered in interviews. I take pride that this book is the first serious research into Sugihara to make extensive use of extant historical materials.

The figure of Sugihara Chiune depicted in the historical record does not contradict that of the humanitarian. Rather, I believe that the addition of the image of the peerless intelligence officer to that of the great humanitarian already described brings us closer to a faithful depiction of the man.

This book is based on historical documents. Because I want it to be accessible to general readers, particularly those of younger generations, I have avoided quoting the originals directly, since today's readership may find them rather difficult to understand; instead, I have chosen to recast them in an easy-to-understand form.

In the past, I worked for about ten years as a part-time university lecturer. Each year, when I took up Sugihara as a topic of study, the students were increasingly eager to listen, and their enthusiasm was a great motivator for me in writing this book. Young people these days tend to be reticent about giving voice to their hopes and dreams. Hopefully, this book will provide them with food for thought when they ponder their futures.

The opinions expressed in this book are my own and do not represent those of the institution where I work.

CHAPTER ONE

The Making of
an Intelligence Officer

Encounter with the Russian Language

Fate and chance impact all our lives. What would have happened if we had not been at a certain place at a certain time, or had not met a certain person? The subject of this book was no exception. The life of Sugihara Chiune, a diplomat and one of the greatest intelligence officers Japan has ever produced, was filled with strange instances of fate and chance. After all, he had not originally aspired to become a diplomat.

Sugihara was born in Gifu prefecture on January 1, 1900, the second son in a family of four boys and one girl, to Sugihara Yoshimi, who worked in a taxation office, and his wife, Yatsu. His father wanted him to become a doctor, given his excellent academic performance, but the young Chiune liked the English language and wanted to find work where he could make the most of his linguistic skills. People with exceptional talents tend to exhibit them from an early age, and Sugihara was no exception, displaying in his teens a linguistic flair that would later enable him to master Russian and several other languages. In his later years, when the subject of which language he found most difficult was raised at the dinner table, someone would invariably interpose, laughingly, "Japanese!"

After his father's wishes, Sugihara sat for a medical school entrance exam, but submitted blank answer sheets as a foolproof way of ensuring failure. His father, well aware of how good his son's academic record usually was, questioned the results, at which point Sugihara's ruse came to light. To escape his father's wrath, he fled to Tokyo, for all intents and purposes leaving home. Wanting to work where he could use languages, he enrolled in the spring of 1918 in the English Department of the Waseda University Higher Normal School (now the School of Education). Knowing that he could not expect to receive financial support from his father after so blatantly disregarding his wishes, Sugihara determined to support himself by working part time, but it soon became clear that he could not make enough to cover his school fees and living expenses. Just when matters had come to a head, chance intervened for the first time. Toward the end of May 1919, he happened across a newspaper article about the Foreign Ministry (Gaimushō) recruiting cadets to study languages abroad. If selected, he would be able to continue his linguistic studies while receiving a salary. However, the entrance exams for that year were scheduled to start on July 3, giving him just a month to prepare, and what's more, they covered a broad range of subjects in addition to languages, including law, economics, and history.

Sugihara was determined to surmount these difficulties and started cramming furiously. The following year he was asked to write an article for *Juken to gakusei* (Examinations and students), a magazine aimed at students preparing for entrance examinations. Titled "Yuki no Harubin yori: Gaimushō ryūgakusei shiken gōkaku dan" (From snowy Harbin: Passing the Foreign Ministry's exams for studying abroad), it appeared in the April 1920 issue, and was reproduced by Watanabe Katsumasa in his book *Shinsō: Sugihara biza* (The truth: Sugihara's visas). In the article, Sugihara spoke of the efforts he made preparing for the exam and laid out a packed study schedule for himself which he followed scrupulously.[1]

	Before Noon	After Noon
Monday	economics	history
Tuesday	international law	economics
Wednesday	international jurisprudence	history
Thursday	international law	legal theory
Friday	history	international law
Saturday	economics	legal theory
Sunday	English	(break)

That year there were thirty-nine candidates for the exam. All passed the first stage, a physical checkup on July 3. This was followed by subject exams,

---

1   Watanabe Katsumasa, *Shinsō: Sugihara biza* [The truth: Sugihara's visas] (Tokyo: Taisho Shuppan, 2000), p. 395.

beginning on July 5 with essays to be written in Japanese and foreign languages, together with comprehension tests in English and German, and continuing on July 7, after a day's break, with a dictation test in English and German and an oral examination. It was no doubt even more of an ordeal than Sugihara had imagined. The results of this first round of exams were announced on July 8, and Sugihara's name was among those who had passed. Excellent linguist as he was, he must have already mastered German as well as English by this time. The second round began the next day, with legal theory and fundamentals of international law, followed on July 10 with general economics and world history. The rigorous exams took almost one week to complete.

Successful candidates would be notified within ten days and receive a certificate to that effect, but if no such communication were received, it meant failure. It is easy to imagine how difficult that wait must have been. Around a week after the exams, Sugihara received a letter telling him to report to the Section of Protocol and Personnel at the Foreign Ministry at 2 p.m. on July 17. This did not follow the official procedure, and Sugihara must have felt somewhat anxious as he headed to the Ministry. Once there, he and the other candidates were briefed as to why they had been summoned. Though the Ministry had intended to appoint eighteen foreign-language cadets that year, only fourteen had reached the required standard. They were told they had not been sent official notification of their success, but rather had been called to the Ministry because there was an imbalance in the languages they wanted to specialize in, and the situation needed to be sorted out. That year a disproportionate number of students had elected to do Spanish, and only a few had chosen Chinese and Russian. Thus, they were each asked to think again about the language they wanted to take up and to write down three languages in order of preference. The Ministry would then do its best to allocate courses accordingly.

The reason for the predominance of Spanish is easily understood when we consider that the year was 1919. The First World War had ended the previous year and the Paris Peace Conference was then in session. This gave Poland, a country with which Sugihara was later to be closely connected, its independence. Japan endorsed the decision and established diplomatic relations with Poland the same year.

Sino-Japanese relations were by no means good, neither during the Great War nor after. During the war, Japan pressured the Chinese government with a set of twenty-one demands. In particular, Japan wanted to take over, in their entirety, the concessions the German Empire had received from China in the Shandong Peninsula. The resulting tide of ill-will toward Japan in China culminated in 1919 in the anti-Japanese protests known as the May Fourth Movement. These events appear to have dissuaded candidates from choosing Chinese, since working in China was potentially dangerous. Sugihara himself wrote of the danger of being in a country where there were frequent anti-Japanese protests. Another reason he gave for the paucity of cadets wishing to take up Chinese was that "because people intrinsically seek after beauty, they prefer to write smoothly with a pen horizontally."[2] This is an extremely interesting analysis, as it implies that Chinese wasn't popular because it was written vertically. Sugihara would have had no idea that in the future he would sign his name time after time in the vertical Japanese script on the large numbers of visas he issued to Jewish refugees.

The other unpopular language was Russian, probably because the Russian Revolution had broken out two years previously, in 1917, climaxing in the October Revolution, and the country remained in turmoil. In 1918, the Bolsheviks brutally murdered Tsar Nicholas II, the last Romanov monarch (who had visited Japan as Crown Prince), his family, and even the family dog. The Tsar's last words were grief-stricken: "What, what?" Russian participation in the First World War had ended with the Bolshevik government unilaterally signing the Treaty of Brest-Litovsk with the Central Powers on March 3, 1918. In response, the Allied countries, Japan included, suspended diplomatic relations with Russia. It was unsurprising in these circumstances that very few wanted to study Russian.

Sugihara, too, had first selected Spanish as his language of choice, but knowing there was only one slot available, he "reluctantly" switched to Russian.[3] However, by the following year, when he wrote "From snowy Harbin," he had come to realize that the study of Russian was of vital

---

2   Watanabe, *Shinsō: Sugihara biza*, p. 411.

3   Ibid.

importance to Japan's present and its future, and should not be neglected. All the same, if that year there had been sufficient cadets taking up Russian (and Chinese) to allow him his first choice, Spanish, his later life would doubtless have been completely different. As we will see, the fact that he learned Russian was of incalculable significance for Japan.

Russian Language Specialist

Japan did not have diplomatic relations with the revolutionary government of Russia when Sugihara became a language cadet at the Foreign Ministry, so it was impossible for him to study in Russia itself. In fact, Japan and Bolshevik Russia were in a virtual state of war in the Far East: Japan, with other Allied Powers, had sent troops into Siberia to intervene in the revolution. How could Russian be studied in such circumstances? In this context, I would like to mention George F. Kennan, the eminent American diplomat and specialist in Soviet affairs.

The United States was one of the last countries to establish diplomatic relations with the Soviet Union, not doing so until 1933. As a result, Kennan studied Russian in Estonia and Latvia, which were formerly part of the Russian Empire. He began his linguistic studies in July 1928 in Tallinn, the capital of Estonia, and found himself fascinated by the rich expressive power of the Russian language. The following year, he moved to Riga in Latvia. From these listening posts close to the Soviet Union, he heard of Stalin's First Five-Year Plan, adopted in 1928, and its commitment to the collectivization of agriculture, and he enthusiastically discussed with colleagues its chances of success.

In contrast, Sugihara was sent to Harbin, in what was then Manchuria and is now called Dongbei (a region in northeastern China). Harbin was a city essentially built by the Russians in 1898, following the construction of the Russian-financed Chinese Eastern Railway, a T-shaped line across Manchuria linking the Trans-Siberian Railway to Vladivostok via Chita, intersecting with a southern spur line from Harbin to Port Arthur. Harbin's central location made the Russians choose it as the base of administration of the railway. Following Japan's victory in the Russo-Japanese War of 1904–1905, Russia ceded most of the southern branch, which became known as the South Manchuria Railway (SMR). Following the Russian Revolution of 1917, large numbers of White Russians moved to Harbin. They had adopted the sobriquet "White" in contrast to the "Red" associated with the revolutionary government they opposed. The presence of a large Russian population made Harbin an ideal place to study the Russian language.

According to "From snowy Harbin," there were no specialist schools teaching Russian at the time. Sugihara therefore boarded with a Russian family to get acquainted with the language and engaged a private tutor to help him with the grammar. When he had business at the Japanese consulate-general, he noticed the large numbers of Russians who came there to apply for visas. Surprised at how few people at the consulate seemed able to understand Russian, he realized just how important the language was and determined to master it.

He paused his studies in November 1920 when he enlisted in the army as a one-year volunteer and was posted to the 12th Company of the 79th Infantry Regiment in Korea, based in Yongsan, now a part of Seoul. According to a telegram dated December 2, 1921, sent to Watanabe Shin'ichi, second secretary in the Oral Examination Section at the Foreign Ministry, Sugihara had completed his year of voluntary service at the end of November. However, on December 1, he was ordered to report for a 120-day training course to be an officer in the reserve corps, and so did not expect to return to his studies until April 1922. Though in later years Sugihara often felt revulsion over the army's tyrannical behavior, the army seems to have appreciated him.

As the need for specialist Russian language training became increasingly apparent, the Japan-Russia Association[4] opened the School of the Japan-Russia Association (Nichiro Kyōkai Gakkō) in September 1920, a specialist training school (*senmon gakkō* under the prewar system) under Foreign Ministry jurisdiction. In 1933, it was renamed Harubin Gakuin (Harbin Institute). Those from the Ministry specializing in the Russian language

---

4   The Japan-Russia Association (Nichiro Kyōkai) was founded in Tokyo in 1906 to promote friendly relations with Russia. In the 1920s, it contributed to the reestablishment of diplomatic relations with Russia and supported Russia-related activities in Manchuria. Its leadership included businessmen, officials of the SMR, and senior navy and army officers. —Trans.

studied here, and Sugihara joined them in September 1922, following the completion of his military service at the end of March. Since the Foreign Ministry was responsible for the school, it received student records, which still exist and allow us to trace Sugihara's progress.[5]

Sugihara Chiune around the time he entered the Foreign Ministry. (Courtesy of NPO Chiune Sugihara Visa for Life)

He took exams immediately after his admission to the school and earned a score of 80 or above for all his seven subjects, including essay writing, Russian-to-Japanese translation, Japanese-to-Russian translation, and conversation. He also received As for health, conduct, and scholastic aptitude. An addendum notes that he had been living with a Russian family until that September and was studying Russian with them. Among the set of exams he took in February and March of the following year, 1923, there was one that required a recitation in Russian. His report made special mention of the fact that he alone provided a synopsis bringing the main points together, demonstrating his meticulous preparation. Even his delivery was in the mode of a public address. His attitude, intonation, and pronunciation were all of the highest standard. Overall, the result was near perfection. His ideas were also deemed of the greatest interest and his future was promising. Given this general evaluation, if Sugihara continued to progress at this rate, his appointment as a consular clerk (*shokisei*)[6] after completing his three years of study was all but guaranteed.

Around this time, it became apparent that gathering all the cadets studying Russian under one roof in Harbin was not necessarily conducive to

---

5 *Reports of examination results in Russian for Foreign Ministry language cadets, Harbin*, Records of the Japanese Ministry of Foreign Affairs: Series 6.1.7.6.3.1 (Personnel affairs: Posts, Asia, examinations, students sent abroad by the government. Reports of examination results), vol. 1.

6 The Foreign Ministry had two entry levels: the elite track, which manned the diplomatic service, and the non-elite track of minor diplomats or consular officials. This second track was divided into *ryūgakusei* (students of foreign languages financed to study abroad) and *shokisei* (clerks), who acted as interpreters and in other area-specific roles. See Barbara J. Brooks, *Japan's Imperial Diplomacy* (Honolulu: University of Hawaii Press, 2000), p. 52. —Trans.

their language studies. Realizing this, Sugihara had put forward his wish to transfer his base of study to Manzhouli, close to the Russian border. The Japanese consul-general in Harbin, Yamauchi Shirō, forwarded his request to Foreign Minister Uchida Yasuya on February 5, and permission was received a month later on March 5. Sugihara left Harbin on March 30, arriving in Manzhouli the following day. There he pursued his study of Russian and, in a test conducted by the consular agent there, earned a score of 90 in Russian, superior to students one or two years his senior.

Marriage to a White Russian

Sugihara was appointed *shokisei* and formally entered the Foreign Ministry on February 8, 1924. At about the same time, his private life underwent a great change with his marriage to Klaudia Apollonova. Unfortunately, nothing is known about the circumstances surrounding his meeting with this attractive White Russian three years younger than himself, as no relevant documents or recollections from those involved have been found. However, it is not particularly strange that Sugihara, Russian enthusiast as he was, should have thrown himself into White Russian society to learn the language, and have made close contacts there.

At that time, the foreign minister's permission was necessary for marriage with a non-Japanese. Sugihara submitted the marriage registration document to the foreign ministry on February 15, just one week after his official appointment. Confirmation finally came ten months later, on December 26, from the then foreign minister Shidehara Kijūrō. Japan and Russia had yet to establish diplomatic relations, and it can be imagined that it was no easy matter to approve a marriage with a Russian, even a White Russian. However, diplomatic relations with Russia resumed on January 20, 1925, with the signing of the Soviet-Japanese Basic Convention. Progress toward this agreement in previous months must have eased the way for the Ministry to approve the marriage.

Sugihara's marriage to a White Russian reflected the trust he had won among the White Russian community in Harbin. It is not difficult to imagine that his marriage with Klaudia formed part of the context in which he became involved in intelligence.

Hazardous Duties

Ordinarily, official records rarely contain information about the activities of early career diplomats, so we are forced to rely on oral testimony or memoirs, which must then be verified. However, in Sugihara's case, such an official document does exist. Compiled in 1937, just over a decade after he joined the Foreign Ministry, it is a unique and valuable record of his work and development in this period. In late 1936, he had been appointed second secretary-interpreter at the Japanese embassy in Moscow, but, unusually, had been refused an entry visa by the Soviet authorities. The report, entitled "Sugihara tsūyakkan no tai-hakkei rojin sesshoku jijō" (Concerning the Contacts with White Russians of Interpreter (Official) Sugihara), is a compilation of relevant information made at that time. Containing a chronological resume of Sugihara's duties from the time he entered the Ministry, it is a valuable reference for details of his early career.

The Japanese consul-general in Harbin at the time of Sugihara's first appointment was Yamauchi Shirō. Sugihara's main duty was to mediate disputes between Japanese and Russians. His excellent Russian skills must therefore have been employed from the very beginning of his career. During the time of Yamauchi's successor, Amō Eiji, in 1925–1927, Sugihara was already undertaking intelligence work, collecting political information, approaching Communist-supporting journalists, and doing background checks on Soviet citizens wishing to visit Japan. Of special mention is a report he compiled in 1927 entitled "Sobieto renpō kokumin keizai taikan" (General survey of the national economy of the Soviet Union). This was a multi-faceted study whose importance was recognized by the Foreign Ministry, which printed and bound it for internal distribution. The preface makes it clear that it was Sugihara, "clerk in the Harbin consulate-general," who had compiled it. The volume, preserved in the Diplomatic Archives of the Ministry of Foreign Affairs, is a bulky work, consisting of over 600 B5-sized pages. Sugihara was only twenty-seven when he produced it. Amō Eiji and the staff at the consulate-general in Harbin, as well as the staff in the First Section of the European and American Bureau of the Foreign Ministry, who were responsible for the Soviet Union, must have been surprised at this emergent young talent and held high hopes for him.

During Amō's tenure as consul-general, Sugihara was ordered to Beijing to examine documents seized in April 1927 from a raid on the Soviet embassy there by police loyal to the warlord Zhang Zuolin (Chang Tso-lun). Zhang had started off as a member of a bandit gang, and during the Russo-Japanese War engaged in spying activities for the Russian army. Captured by the Japanese and sentenced to death as a spy, he was saved at the last moment by Major Tanaka Giichi (who would later become prime minister of Japan) and, based on this experience, he would go on to have close relations with Japan. Taking advantage of the Xinhai Revolution (in 1911), he built himself a power base in Fengtian (Mukden, now Shenyang) in

The report titled "Sobieto renpō kokumin keizai taikan" (General survey of the national economy of the Soviet Union), written by Sugihara as a clerk in the Harbin consulate-general.

central Manchuria, and following Yuan Shikai's fall from power in 1916, he took control of the army and government there. His pro-Japanese sentiments were underscored when he recruited Japanese advisers and clamped down on anti-Japanese activities in Fengtian during the height of the May Fourth Movement. He was strongly anti-Communist, and not only Japan but the United States and countries in Europe looked upon him favorably. He captured Beijing in July 1926, and a year later, in the face of advancing Nationalist troops, proclaimed himself Generalissimo of the Republic of China. He combined his forces with those of other warlords but was forced to retreat.

The National Revolutionary Army (NRA) under Chiang Kai-shek began its Northern Expedition in June 1926 to eliminate the warlords in northern China. In March 1927, its troops reached Nanjing, raiding several foreign consulates, attacking and looting foreign interests in the city, and killing a number of foreigners. The foreign powers were concerned about the degree of what they perceived as Soviet influence in the army and, fearing that

Beijing might suffer the same fate as Nanjing, they demanded that Zhang Zuolin, as the person in control, eliminate Soviet influence from that city. The next month, as we have seen, his adherents raided the Soviet embassy, arrested a number of Russians and Chinese Communists, and seized documents, including leaflets. The fact that Sugihara was sent to examine these documents is a testament that his skill in Russian and his capabilities in the intelligence field had already been recognized by his superiors.

Sugihara continued to have the same general duties—collecting political intelligence, making approaches to journalists, and checking the credentials of Soviet citizens—under the next consul-general, Yagi Motohachi, as he had had under Amō, but he was also involved in the most delicate matter of his career so far, a plan to extract a cipher book from the Soviet consulate in Harbin. A member of the Soviet consular staff who held the key to the safe where the book was kept had apparently offered to sell the key to the Japanese. Sugihara appears to have twice met with him in secret. At the time, acquiring the codes and cipher patterns to decipher the telegrams sent by the other side was one of the most consuming tasks among intelligence officers. This episode speaks of the intensity of the intelligence war between Japan and the Soviet Union that was conducted far from the public view.

A further incident is also of interest. Yagi had been contacted by Kawasumi Tadao, the acting consul-general in Khabarovsk, concerning a Russian called Chernyak who had escaped from Khabarovsk, and he asked Sugihara to look after him. The fugitive was probably counting on Japan to buy important information from the Soviet side. Sugihara used the expression "enigmatic Russian" to describe him, suggesting he was a somewhat risky individual. He reported that he was running this man as a secret agent, which suggests not only that Yagi trusted Sugihara to take charge of this suspicious character, but also that Sugihara was continuing to make steady strides as an intelligence officer in Japanese-Soviet matters.

Meeting Ōhashi Chūichi

Perhaps the most important event in Sugihara's time at the consulate in Harbin was his meeting in 1931 with the new consul-general, Ōhashi Chūichi, who, impressed with Sugihara's abilities, arranged his transfer to the Foreign Affairs Department of the State of Manchuria (Manchukuo) in 1932. This was to become a major turning point in Sugihara's life.

Ōhashi, regarded as something of a swashbuckler by the Japanese Foreign Ministry, was seven years Sugihara's senior, having been born in 1893. In 1918, the year before Sugihara passed the Foreign Ministry examination for language cadets, Ōhashi had graduated from the Imperial University of Tokyo (today the University of Tokyo) in British Law and passed the Foreign Ministry examination for diplomats. Incidentally, in the same cohort was Ōtaka Shōjirō, who was the Japanese minister to Latvia, Estonia, and Lithuania when Sugihara was vice-consul in Kaunas. Ōhashi was first posted to Mukden (Fengtian) for just over a year and then spent almost eight years, until 1927, in various cities in the United States. After that, he headed the Third Section of the Foreign Ministry's Bureau of Commercial Affairs and in 1930 was appointed first secretary at the Japanese legation in China, returning to China after an absence of some ten years. In June 1931, just three months before the Manchurian Incident (see next page), he was made consul-general in Harbin, becoming Sugihara's superior. Morishima Morito, the consul in Mukden at that time, described Ōhashi as "a rare kind of diplomat by Foreign Ministry standards." Morishima became Japan's minister to Portugal during the Second World War and was a Socialist member of the House of Representatives after the war. All the same, he cannot be said to have followed the orthodox path as a diplomat.

The mainstream Foreign Ministry diplomacy at this time centered on Shidehara Kijūrō, who was to serve four terms as foreign minister, and the foreign policy Japan followed at the time is referred to as "Shidehara diplomacy." This has long been characterized as a peaceful diplomacy based on international cooperation, but today's scholarly understanding is more nuanced. It was in fact Morishima Morito who, early in the postwar period, first drew attention

Ōhashi Chūichi. (Diplomatic Archives of the Ministry of Foreign Affairs, Japan)

to issues concerning Shidehara diplomacy as it was practiced at the time of the Manchurian Incident.[7] In this sense, he showed remarkable foresight. Morishima was what we may call a "China hand," having been based in that country for a long period. His criticism of Shidehara may be largely ascribed to his dissatisfaction over the fact that those with a thorough knowledge of Chinese affairs had been sidelined when Shidehara, who had never served in China, became foreign minister, and that the most influential figures in the Ministry were the European and American experts Shidehara favored. Morishima criticized Shidehara's China policy as stressing principles over reality. Nevertheless, they both wanted to promote good relations with China. Ōhashi, on the other hand, held a completely different view.

On September 18, 1931, just three months after Ōhashi's arrival in Harbin, an explosion occurred on the SMR line near Mukden and was ascribed to Chinese forces. This is known as the Manchurian (or Mukden) Incident. It had been engineered by the Kwantung Army, a force originally set up to protect the SMR and the Japanese concession in the Guandong (Kwantung) Peninsula, to create a pretext for sending troops outside the railway zone into Manchuria proper. The Army General Staff in Tokyo fiercely opposed such moves by the Kwantung Army, fearing that the situation would spread into northern Manchuria and escalate into a confrontation with Soviet troops.

Morishima, as consul in Mukden, was told of the explosion on the night of September 18 and ordered to report to the Special Service Group (Tokumu Kikan) there. He arrived to find, among others, Colonel Itagaki Seishirō, senior deputy chief of staff for operations/intelligence in the Kwantung Army, and Major Hanaya Tadashi, head of the Office. He tried to reason with them that the matter should be resolved through diplomatic negotiations rather than military action, but they chastised him for his interference. Major Hanaya even unsheathed his sword and demanded to know whether Morishima was interfering in the authority of the Supreme Command. Unsurprisingly, Morishima later titled his memoirs *Inbō, ansatsu, guntō* (Plots, assassinations, swords).

---

7   Morishima Morito, *Inbō, ansatsu, guntō: Ichi gaikōkan no kaisō* [Plots, assassinations, swords: Memoirs of a diplomat] (Tokyo: Iwanami Shoten, 1950).

In contrast to the other consular officials, Ōhashi, aligning himself with the Kwangtung Army, strongly urged that troops be sent to Harbin as a strategic site in northern Manchuria. Amakasu Masahiko, a former captain of the military police who murdered the anarchist Ōsugi Sakae and others in the aftermath of the 1923 Great Kanto earthquake, was sent to Harbin by the Kwantung Army to organize anti-Japanese actions there and so provide an excuse for sending in troops. Ōhashi responded by requesting that troops be sent to Harbin to maintain security. His actions identified him as a Kwantung Army sympathizer within the Foreign Ministry and the champion of the army's advance into northern Manchuria.

Straying into a Nest of Communists

Why did the maverick Ōhashi promote Sugihara to such a degree? As we shall see, Sugihara was opposed to the events of the Manchurian Incident and was unwilling to aid the Kwantung Army. What was it that connected two people so different in principle and mode of action?

It may be that Ōhashi took Sugihara under his wing because they both hailed from Gifu Prefecture, but if that were the only reason, it would throw doubt on Ōhashi's acumen. What was it that he detected in the talented Sugihara? To answer this, we can refer again to the aforementioned 1937 Sugihara Report, where we find details of a trip the two made together into Soviet territory. This report mentions in an almost offhand way that while in Vladivostok, they strayed by mistake into the International Seamen's Club (Interclub), a Japanese Communist Party den, and were almost discovered there by party members.

At that time, the Japanese Communist Party was illegal in Japan and accordingly suppressed. The savage crackdown by the state on March 15, 1928, was described in an eponymous and chilling short story by Kobayashi Takiji, an author whose works have recently enjoyed a resurgence in popularity. The large number of Communists arrested and tortured and the considerable loss of life described in the story are based on fact. Further arrests were made on April 16 the following year. Kobayashi himself was arrested as a Communist and died a cruel death in jail in 1933.

Should the Harbin consul-general and a member of his staff have been found inside a Communist hangout, the situation could have quickly turned nasty, since they represented the face of the hated government. If it were truly as Sugihara had reported, that they had wandered into the Club in error, it is strange that Sugihara was neither reprimanded nor subjected to disciplinary action for involving his superior in such a risky situation. Perhaps Ōhashi had asked Sugihara, fluent in Russian and conversant with the situation in Vladivostok, to take him to the Club to inquire into Soviet activities regarding Japan. This would explain why Sugihara was not censured for taking Ōhashi to the Club and reveals a side of Ōhashi not previously described. It might also be part of the reason he trusted Sugihara. In other words, Ōhashi was, above all, a person who appreciated the importance of intelligence and the efforts of his staff. If he had been a run-of-the-mill consul-general, he may, if necessary, have ordered a subordinate to enter a hangout of Japanese Communists, but he would never have gone himself. Though this does not excuse such an imprudent action, it does show that he was not the type to expose his subordinates to danger by themselves, and this estimation of his character is backed by Morishima's comment that he was full of human warmth and moved more by emotion and duty than by reason. No wonder he was regarded as a maverick in the world of diplomacy.

It is hardly surprising that Sugihara, an intelligence officer whose reputation depended on recognizing the importance of the information he managed to obtain, found it easy to like someone like Ōhashi, who was willing to personally face danger with him.

CHAPTER TWO

The Manchurian Government Foreign Affairs Department and the Chinese Eastern Railway

A Lost Scenario

The leading voice in Soviet diplomacy in the 1920s and 1930s was Maxim Litvinov. In the prewar Soviet Union, the term "people's commissar" was used for the rank known in other countries as "minister." Thus the People's Commissariat of Foreign Affairs (Narkomindel, 1917–1946) was headed by a People's Commissar for Foreign Affairs, assisted by a Deputy People's Commissar. In 1921, Litvinov was appointed First Deputy People's Commissar of Foreign Affairs, and in 1930, People's Commissar of Foreign Affairs. He hammered out a line of cooperation with European countries, and in 1934 facilitated the acceptance of the Soviet Union into the League of Nations. Later he spoke of Japanese-Soviet relations in this period.

> The friendliest relationship between the Soviet Union and Japan existed in the period between the resumption of diplomatic relations (1925) and the Manchurian Incident (1931). There were no conflicts or deep misunderstandings, and even if disputes arose, they were resolved peacefully through diplomatic means. Neither side issued threats. However, the hitherto-friendly Japanese-Soviet relations came to an end with the Manchurian Incident.[8]

The Manchurian Incident was originally a conflict between Japan and China, so it may seem surprising that it brought about an abrupt change in Japanese-Soviet relations. All the same, this breakdown in relations that Litvinov alludes to impacted Sugihara's life as a diplomat in a major way.

These matters may be traced back to the Russo-Japanese Convention

---

8   Jane Degras, ed., *Soviet Documents on Foreign Policy, vol. III, 1933–1941* (London: Oxford University Press, 1951), p. 57.

of 1907, signed just two years after the conclusion of the Russo-Japanese War. It had both public and secret clauses, the latter reaffirming both countries' spheres of influence in Manchuria. The northern half of Manchuria, centered on the Chinese Eastern Railway (CER), was deemed to lie in the Russian sphere and the southern half, centered on the South Manchuria Railway (SMR), in Japan's sphere. This division had been made without any consultation with China. The secret agreement was extended after relations between Japan and the Soviet Union were normalized in 1925.

The CER has been written in Japanese in different ways at different times, but "Chinese Eastern Railway" (*Chūtō tetsudō*) was generally used around the time of the Manchurian Incident. Then, on June 1, 1933, the name was changed to "North Manchuria Railway" (*Hokuman tetsudō*).[9] Sugihara was to be deeply involved in the Japanese-Soviet negotiations concerning the purchase of this railway.

The Manchurian Incident, presented as an attack by the Chinese on the SMR, a Japanese concession, was a pretext for the Kwantung Army to take action against Chinese forces. As is well known today, the attack was, in fact, engineered by the Kwantung Army. The army leadership in Tokyo fundamentally approved this reckless act but strictly forbade any intrusion into northern Manchuria, recognized as within the Soviet sphere of influence. The Soviets' response to the event was to avoid getting involved. The Soviet Union was still regarded as an outsider in the international community, and it was wary of aligning itself with the many countries that criticized Japan's aggression, fearing that they might make an abrupt policy turn, settle their differences with Japan, and turn on the Soviet Union. Given the instability of its international standing, it had to tread very carefully with regard to the Incident.

At the time of the Incident, the army leadership, headed by Army Minister Minami Jirō and Chief of the General Staff Kanaya Hanzō, and government leaders like Prime Minister Wakatsuki Reijirō and Foreign Minister Shidehara Kijūrō concurred in opposing any dispatch of troops to northern Manchuria for fear of igniting a war with the Soviet Union. At this

---

9   We will continue to use CER in this book as it is the standard English usage. —Ed.

point, therefore, the interests of both sides, including those of the Japanese army, were strangely in accord.

Both Minami and Kanaya were under the influence of General Ugaki Kazushige, then governor-general of Korea, who wielded extensive power in the army behind the scenes. Ugaki had long had close relations with the Minseitō (Constitutional Democratic Party), then in power with Wakatsuki as prime minister. The Minseitō had developed out of the Kenseikai (Constitutional Politics Association) and was one of the two principal political parties, the other being the Seiyūkai (Constitutional Friendship Association). Ugaki had served as army minister in three Kenseikai/Minseitō cabinets between 1924–1927 and again in 1929–1930. A cooperative relationship developed between the mainstream army faction Ugaki headed and the Minseitō over restraining the advance of the Kwantung Army into northern Manchuria. In 1931, the Minseitō had an absolute majority in the Lower House. Given the party's relationship with Ugaki's faction, the Kwantung Army felt betrayed on a number of occasions. If this relationship had continued over the long term, there is a strong possibility that the Manchurian Incident would have been resolved early on, the situation would have returned to normal with League of Nations approval, and Manchukuo would not have attained independence. This is not just my view, by the way, since Banno Junji, emeritus professor of the University of Tokyo and a leading scholar in modern Japanese political history, also described this eventuality as a "lost scenario."

With cooperation between the Ugaki faction and the Minseitō, the political situation seemed as if it would stabilize, but a faction within the party, led by Home Minister Adachi Kenzō, argued that the emergency situation called for a coalition with the Seiyūkai, the opposition party. His faction clashed violently with Wakatsuki's ruling faction, which supported a one-party cabinet; the cabinet fell into disunity and resigned en masse on December 11, 1931. Two days later, it was replaced by the Seiyūkai cabinet of Inukai Tsuyoshi. Though the Seiyūkai was a party that ostensibly followed fundamental constitutional principles, Inukai appointed as army minister Araki Sadao, a member of the hard-line faction within the army who opposed Ugaki's faction. The restraints placed on the Kwantung Army were lifted and, in an instant, the flames of the Manchurian Incident spread to northern Manchuria. Harbin, where Sugihara was living, was taken by the Kwantung Army on February 5, 1932.

The Turning Point in Japanese-Soviet Relations

The change of government in Tokyo meant that the Soviet Union could no longer just turn a blind eye to the Manchurian Incident, and from the end of 1931 into the following year, it repeatedly proposed a nonaggression pact with Japan to counterbalance its distrust of the country. I will deal with this in more detail below, as it is an extremely important issue in regard to Japanese-Soviet relations at the time.

As the effects of the Manchurian Incident spread to northern Manchuria, the rise in tension between Japan and the Soviet Union had an impact on Sugihara's work as well. For example, he was ordered to draft a rebuttal in French of the report issued by the Lytton Commission, the fact-finding mission headed by the Englishman Victor Bulwer-Lytton (Lord Lytton) that visited Manchuria in 1932 at the request of the League of Nations. Sugihara appears to have been fluent enough in French by that time to be entrusted with drafting a document on which Japan's future depended.

Sugihara had been negative about the Manchurian Incident from the first. An interesting episode concerning this attitude was the issue of transporting the Kwantung Army troops on the eastern section of the CER. According to the 1937 Sugihara Report, he acted as an interpreter for Hyakutake Haruyoshi and Doihara Kenji, heads of the Harbin and Mukden Special Service Group respectively, when they were in talks with CER authorities. Worth noting is that Sugiahara deliberately added the word "intimidating" in describing the attitude of the Japanese side.

According to another Foreign Ministry archival source, after the Kwantung Army occupied Harbin, defeated Chinese troops fled into the eastern section of the CER zone and pillaged Japanese assets at Imenpo (Yimianpo), an area just over 100 miles east of Harbin, threatening security. On February 21, 1932, the Kwantung Army ordered Hyakutake to request CER authorities to permit its troops to be transported using the eastern branch of the line if it proved necessary to protect Japanese residents in the zone. The Soviet administrators of the line promised to notify Moscow right away and would permit troop transport if Moscow gave its approval but refused to do so on the grounds that Moscow had not responded. When negotiations by Hyakutake on February 24 and Doihara the following day failed to resolve this impasse, the Japanese ambassador to Moscow, Hirota Kōki,[10] took up the issue with Lev Karakhan, Deputy People's Commissar for Foreign Affairs (Litvinov was then at the Conference on Disarmament in Geneva). He was successful in securing the required permission late at night on February 27, albeit as a special exception.

The Soviet side had expressed doubts about the legality of using the railway to transport troops, based on the provisions of the Portsmouth Treaty and its successor, the Soviet-Japanese Basic Convention. Article 7 of the Portsmouth Treaty stated that Japan and Russia could use their respective railways in Manchuria only for commercial and industrial purposes and prohibited their use for military ends. Hirota contended that the use of the railway for troop transport was purely defensive, because its purpose was to protect the lives and property of Japanese residents in the region, and had no military intent. He added that the appropriate fares would be paid for the troops and that this was within the province of CER operations.

A Man of Principle

It is generally understood that, given the lack of headway in talks in Harbin over troop access to the CER, it was Hirota's tact that brought success and achieved the concession from the Soviet Union. However, what Sugihara saw was Hyakutake's and Doihara's "intimidating" demeanor. This word merits attention. It is thought the report "Concerning the Contacts with White Russians of Interpreter (Official) Sugihara" was compiled around March 15, 1937. Let us look at the situation at that time.

The previous year, an attempted coup d'état, the most serious in Japanese history, had taken place on February 26. Based on the date, it is known as

---

10 Hirota was later foreign minister (1933–1936, 1937–1938) and prime minister (1936–1937). After the Second World War, he was tried as a Class A war criminal and was the only civil official to be executed.

the 2-26 Incident. Though it ended in failure, it forced liberals and internationalists to remain silent, through fear of terrorism, as contemporaries and historians have pointed out. The new cabinet subsequently formed by Hirota Kōki expanded the military budget massively, to the astounding extent that it comprised well over half the national budget, around seventy percent. It was at this time, too, that the imperial ordinance *Gunbudaijin gen'eki bukan sei* (Legal requirement for military ministers to be appointed from active duty) was reintroduced. Since only a serving General/Admiral or Lieutenant General/Vice Admiral could become a minister of the army or navy under this ordinance, the military had the power to determine the fate of the cabinet. It was the complete opposite of civilian control. Since serving officers bypassed the cabinet and reported directly to the Emperor, even if the prime minister designated a certain officer for a ministerial position, the military could refuse to release that officer, thereby sabotaging the appointment. And if the military did not like the direction the cabinet was moving, it could withdraw its ministers and topple it.

The first Yamamoto Gonbei cabinet, which came into office in February 1913 following the first constitutional defense movement of 1912–1913, with its slogans "Protect constitutional government" and "Overthrow clan cliques," carried out a large number of reforms, including the abolition of the requirement, introduced in 1900, for military ministers to be serving officers. However, in 1936, during the Hirota cabinet, the military successfully resurrected the old system, using the excuse of preventing ministerial appointments of those generals who had been transferred to the reserve on suspicion of being involved in planning the 2-26 Incident. This gave the military sweeping control over personnel placement, thereby increasing military solidarity.

In January 1937, following a disagreement between the government and the army, Hirota resigned. Ugaki Kazushige was nominated as his successor, in the hope that he, an army man himself, could control the army. However, the army abused the system that had been resurrected and refused to appoint an army minister, thus preventing Ugaki from forming a government. The following month, Hayashi Senjūrō, an army general and admiral, was selected to replace him. Hayashi had been Commanding General of the

Japanese army in Korea at the time of the Manchurian Incident, when he ordered his forces to cross into Manchuria without any authorization from Japan. This earned him the sobriquet "Border-Crossing General" (a general operating beyond his area of responsibility). Ishihara Kanji, a prime mover in the Manchurian Incident, commented, "With General and Admiral Hayashi in power, we will have free rein." In the process of forming his cabinet, however, Hayashi rejected Ishihara's associates. The new government was formed on February 2.

In an environment of growing military power, Sugihara must have been quite strong-principled to have used the word "intimidating" to criticize the army's behavior in his report to the Foreign Ministry, even if it was no more than an internal document. This same harsh criticism also appears in an unfinished account he wrote late in life, where he described professional soldiers as a group as "imprudent, irresponsible, and reckless."[11] His ability to see through the fog of the age he lived in from an inherently liberal perspective was already evident even at this time.

Transfer to the Manchurian Government Foreign Affairs Department

The establishment of the state of Manchuria (Manchukuo) was officially proclaimed on March 1, 1932. Only six months had passed since the Manchurian Incident, and problems of every kind inevitably emerged in the process of establishing the new nation. Though Manchukuo's Foreign Affairs Department had neither facilities nor equipment, Xie Jieshi, who had taken part in negotiations between the warlord of Jilin Province and the Japanese army after the Manchurian Incident, was appointed foreign minister, with Ōhashi Chūichi, the former consul-general in Harbin, as his deputy. Ōhashi had the tricky role of setting the Department up. One of the people he particularly requested the Japanese Foreign Ministry to transfer to the new state was Sugihara.

Sugihara worked in the Department for around three years, until 1935.

---

11 Sugihara Chiune, Ketsudan: Gaikōkan no kaisō [A decision: Memoirs of a diplomat], in *Ketsudan: Inochi no biza* [A decision: Visas to save lives], ed. Watanabe Katsumasa with Sugihara Yukiko (Tokyo: Taisho Shuppan, 1996).

Let us think again about the reasons Ōhashi selected him and why he decided to go. As we have seen, when the consequences of the Manchurian Incident spread to northern Manchuria, the Soviet Union repeatedly proposed a nonaggression pact to counterbalance its distrust of Japan. Soviet Foreign Commissar Maxim Litvinov had first proposed such a pact to Yoshizawa Kenkichi, then ambassador to France since 1930, when he stopped briefly in Moscow in December 1931 on his way back to Japan to become foreign minister in the Inukai cabinet. The same proposal was made more than ten times in 1932, through official and private channels.

Ōhashi's stance on this matter is of great interest. According to Morishima Morito, Ōhashi was of the opinion that such a pact should be immediately and unconditionally concluded to ensure Manchukuo's secure development. Morishima, who had met Ōhashi in Tokyo, was amazed at how passionately he expounded his views to all and sundry.[12]

Ōhashi later worked as vice-foreign minister under Matsuoka Yōsuke and, after the war, published his memoirs,[13] which focused on this time. Right in the preface, he wrote that the greatest mistake of Japanese diplomacy had been the Manchurian Incident and the subsequent establishment of Manchukuo. The lack of self-reflection is astounding. However, it should be noted that he mentioned a further error—that in 1932, the Japanese government continued to refuse proposals for a nonaggression pact with the Soviet Union. Since the book was published in 1952, it appears that his regrets over this were still present twenty years later. In fact, the issue of the nonaggression pact suggests that Ōhashi was not simply a fellow traveler with the Kwangtung Army and the military in general.

Let us look at a few instances of how those responsible for diplomacy at the time responded to Soviet proposals for a nonaggression pact. In a postwar roundtable discussion among people associated with the Foreign Ministry, Yoshizawa Kenkichi, foreign minister in the Inukai cabinet, said that even though he personally thought the pact was worth considering, the power of

---

12 Morishima, *Inbō ansatsu guntō*, pp. 102–3.

13 Ōhashi Chūichi, *Taiheiyō sensō yuraiki: Matsuoka gaikō no shinsō* [The origins of the Pacific War: The truth about Matsuoka Diplomacy] (Tokyo: Kaname shobo, 1952).

the army in 1932 was so great that it failed to receive any attention because of the ferocious opposition of Army Minister Araki Sadao, who had stated rudely, "I have no faith in such a prostitute's pledge." Yoshizawa, pressured by Araki's threatening manner, shelved the matter, intending to reintroduce it when an opportunity presented itself. However, Prime Minister Inukai was assassinated on May 15, and the cabinet resigned en masse, thereby losing Yoshizawa the chance to bring the matter up again.

The assassination of Inukai, known in Japan as the 5-15 Incident, brought party politics to an end. Saitō Makoto, an admiral in the Navy, was chosen as head of a cabinet of national unity. The foreign minister was a veteran diplomat, Uchida Yasuya, who had held the same post under four previous administrations, including that of the assassinated Hara Takashi. At the beginning of his tenure, Uchida also appears to have been keen to conclude the nonaggression pact, as he mentioned when he visited Saionji Kinmochi, two-time prime minister and elder statesman (genrō) with the power to nominate prime ministers. However, Uchida, who had been president of the SMR at the time of the Manchurian Incident, was reduced to being an "army lapdog," merely conveying the opinions of the Kwantung Army to the government. When he became aware of the strength of the army's opposition to a nonaggression pact, he did an about-face and disappointed Saionji, saying it was impossible to conclude a pact due to army opposition. And during his tenure as foreign minister, the Japanese government formally rejected the pact with the Soviet Union on December 13, 1932.

Another person of interest here is Hirota Kōki, ambassador to the Soviet Union from 1930 to 1932, who succeeded Uchida as foreign minister in 1933. The previous year, when he returned to Japan from the Soviet Union, he said something to the *Asahi Shimbun*, a leading daily, that could be interpreted as a statement in favor of a Soviet-Japanese nonaggression pact. Morishima, too, categorized Hirota as a supporter of the pact "as long as certain conditions were met." However, pioneering research by Leonid N. Kutakov,[14] using Soviet sources, reveals that when the topic

---

14 Leonid N. Kutakov, *Istoriya Sovetsko-iaponskikh Diplomaticheskikh Otnoshenii* [History of Soviet-Japanese diplomatic relations] (Moscow: Institut mezhdunarodnykh otnoshenii, 1962).

of a nonaggression pact came up, Ambassador Hirota reacted negatively, saying that all issues between Japan and Russia had been resolved with the Portsmouth Treaty. There is strong supporting evidence for this, in that the Soviets used a variety of routes in their approach to negotiations. There would not have been any need to try other approaches if the most obvious route, to work through the resident Japanese ambassador, had been successful and Hirota had shown a positive attitude.

With so many in Foreign Ministry circles opposed to the nonaggression pact, Ōhashi's enthusiastic support was unusual. Incidentally, Morishima thought that, since it would be difficult for Japan and the Soviet Union to enter into such a pact without going through the proper channels, a better method would be to temporarily conclude one between Manchukuo and the Soviet Union, and then extend it to Japan in stages. He was supported in this by Arita Hachirō, vice-foreign minister under Uchida Yasuya, and Tani Masayuki, head of the Asiatic Bureau in the Foreign Ministry. However, when he mentioned it to Ōhashi, Ōhashi held fast to his position and wouldn't budge.

If we consider only Morishima's memoirs, Ōhashi comes across as a strongly opinionated person. We should not, however, forget that Morishima's account concerning the nonaggression pact was based on observations at a time when both men had just returned to Japan, around November 1932. In a telegram that Ōhashi sent to Vice-Minister Arita on December 12, 1932, after he had returned to Manchukuo, he suggested that a nonaggression pact should be concluded between the Soviet Union and Manchukuo in order to improve relations with the Soviet Union. Later, he and Sugihara were both actively involved in negotiations over the terms of the sale of the CER to Japan. There was a deep-rooted opinion among some segments of the army that there was no need to pay any money for it at all, since it would eventually become Japan's anyway. Ōhashi evaluated Soviet capabilities and was convinced that problems should be solved by diplomatic rather than military means. Such an approach likely appealed to Sugihara, who, as a result, must have regarded Ōhashi as a superior he could trust.

Sugihara's transfer to Manchukuo, which on its face might seem difficult to understand, and his rapport with Ōhashi were sustained by an empathy regarding the fundamentals of Japanese-Soviet diplomacy, as well as a shared sense of what intelligence was.

Negotiations over the CER

It was his work during the negotiations over the sale of the CER that immediately enhanced Sugihara's reputation as an intelligence officer. This railway, basically under joint Chinese and Russian administration, formed a great artery running east and west across Manchuria. With the establishment of Manchukuo, it fell under joint Manchukuo-Soviet administration. However, Manchukuo was not recognized by other countries, including the Soviet Union, and joint administration was made impossible by the lack of diplomatic relations between the two.

It was Hirota Kōki, then Japanese ambassador in Moscow, who decided to tackle the problem. Having obtained Soviet permission to transport Kwantung Army troops along the eastern branch of the CER, he proposed to Lev Karakhan, Deputy People's Commissar for Foreign Affairs, that while it was good to settle such small local issues, it would be even better to resolve a much bigger issue that would significantly improve Japanese-Soviet relations. Karakhan agreed and asked what that might mean in concrete terms. Without hesitation, Hirota suggested selling the CER to Japan/Manchukuo.

The Soviets viewed the proposal positively. Hirota returned to Japan immediately after these meetings, and his return was reported favorably in Japanese newspapers, which cited his success in fishery negotiations and his paving the way for the purchase of the CER. It was at this very time, too, that Hirota advocated a nonaggression pact with the Soviet Union "after resolving pending issues." One of these "pending issues" was, needless to say, the CER.

Though Hirota had laid the groundwork to open negotiations, the Kwantung Army maneuvered to lower the value of the railway itself by various stratagems, such as putting pressure on Russian railway employees and limiting the number of Russian carriages that could enter Manchukuo. These ploys delayed the opening of official negotiations. Hirota's successor as ambassador to Moscow, Ōta Tamekichi, worried about this situation. Extant Foreign Ministry documents provide insight into the efforts made by both sides during Ōta's tenure to improve Japanese-Soviet relations, which had worsened after the Manchurian Incident. The mutual concessions that were reached are a testament to Ōta's sincere character.

In May 1933, the Soviet government officially announced its formal proposal to sell the CER through Ambassador Ōta. The Japanese government decided that the Manchukuo government would be responsible for the purchase and that Japan would act as a mediator to aid the negotiations. The Manchukuo team was led by Ding Shiyuan, the Manchukuo ambassador to Tokyo, and Ōhashi Chūichi, Manchukuo's deputy foreign minister, and included Sugihara Chiune. The Soviet side was headed by Konstantin Yurenev, the Soviet ambassador to Tokyo, and Benedict Ignatiev Kozlovsky, Director of the Second Eastern Department of the Narkomindel.

A Tough Negotiator

The first round of formal negotiations for the sale of the CER was held in Tokyo on June 26, 1933, at the Official Residence of the Vice-Minister of Foreign Affairs, but was confined to an exchange of polite greetings between Foreign Minister Uchida Yasuya, Soviet Ambassador Yurenev, and Manchukuo Ambassador Ding Shiyuan. The second round on June 28 was limited to the Soviet and Manchukuo delegations announcing their general secretaries. Sugihara Chiune was selected for this role by the Manchukuo side, while his Soviet counterpart was Vladimir Jelezniakoff, first secretary of the Soviet embassy in Tokyo.

According to Morishima Morito, Ōhashi's successor in Harbin as consul-general, a key figure in the negotiations on the Soviet side was the Soviet consul-general in Harbin, M. Slavutsky, who had a wealth of knowledge and experience concerning the CER issue. He was 36 or 37 at the time, a good match for Sugihara at 33.

It is very strange that the aforementioned 1937 Sugihara Report makes no mention at all of the CER purchase negotiations. All that appears is that he bore the brunt of negotiations with M. Slavutsky over many issues of varying importance related to Manchukuo-Soviet relations and that he rarely yielded to the Soviet consul-general. This hints that Sugihara was a tough negotiator who stood up to this key Soviet figure.

The third round of talks, held on July 3, was the highlight of the negotiations so far, with both sides proposing the sale price they were willing to
offer or accept. The Soviet delegation demanded 250 million roubles (625
million yen) but the Manchukuo side offered less than one tenth of that,
just fifty million yen, an extreme difference of 12.5 to 1.

Sugihara's turn came in the sixth round, on August 4, when he rebutted
the Soviet demand. He expressed doubts about various fundamental points
regarding the basis on which the Soviets had made their calculation. Besides
pointing out that the economic value of the CER had declined with the
current ongoing expansion of the Manchukuo rail network, he explicitly
stated that its facilities were in a decrepit state.

Nevertheless, regarding the reduction of the Soviet asking price, it would
be unfair not to mention acts of violence committed by Kwantung Army,
such as damaging tracks and derailing trains, that they noisily claimed had
been Soviet acts. Such plots were of the same caliber as those that brought
about the Manchurian Incident in the first place. In September 1933, the
talks foundered when six CER Soviet employees were arrested and imprisoned in Manchukuo. The Soviets did not take this in silence. At the beginning of October, when negotiations had hit a dead end, they published five
telegrams that had been sent to the Japanese government by the Japanese
ambassador to Manchukuo and the Japanese consul-general in Harbin,
concerning a plot to make the Soviets lower the price for the CER, thereby
exposing Japan's intrigues to the world. The telegrams made clear the range
of Japanese who had been involved in the arrests: employees of the Japanese
embassy in Manchukuo, Foreign Ministry officials, and members of the
Kwantung Army's Special Service Group. Soviet newspapers also reported
that the placement of Manchurians in the Soviet employees' former positions
was part of a plan by Japan and Manchukuo to take over the CER. Beyond
the arrests, the telegrams also revealed that Ōhashi had requested that pressure be exerted on the CER to give Japan an advantage in the negotiations
being held in Tokyo. The expression "brutally frank" is very apt here.

This incident was known at the time as the "Fictitious Documents
Affair" (*kaibunsho jiken*): documents of unknown origin intended to slan-
der and expose. The following year, Foreign Minister Hirota, in response

to a question in the House of Representatives, declared that the telegrams should be regarded as *kaibunsho* and that their contents were nonsensical. However, Lieutenant Colonel Suzuki Teiichi, who headed the Army Ministry's Newspaper Group, acknowledged to Harada Kumao, Saionji Kinmochi's secretary, that the Japanese telegrams were genuine and had been stolen by the Soviets. Despite this, the Japanese had no option but to feign anger at the publication of these "unfounded" *kaibunsho*.

How did the Soviets get ahold of the Japanese telegrams? Were they intercepted and deciphered, or had they been secretly photographed? An investigation led by Sakuma Shin, head of the Foreign Ministry's Telegraphic Section, was quickly launched. The diplomatic code, developed with the help of the Navy, was deemed highly reliable, and the investigation determined that, since the code had been introduced just two years previously, there would not have been sufficient samples around to make machine decryption feasible.

This rejection from the first of the possibility that the code had been broken established a poor precedent when we consider Japan's subsequent history, and may well point to an underlying cause of Japan's loss of the intelligence war before and during the Second World War.

Conclusion of the Negotiations

Following the disclosure about the telegrams, the negotiations were suspended for around six months. When they were resumed on February 26, 1934, Ambassador Yurenov reduced the asking price from 625 million yen to 200 million yen in one fell swoop. Sugihara clearly had a hand in this reduction.

Regarding Sugihara's information-gathering activities at this time, we have the testimony of Kasai Tadakazu, a friend who was then studying at the Harbin Institute. According to Kasai, Sugihara used his own intelligence network to investigate various matters within the CER zone including the extent to which the Soviets removed freight cars. This network would naturally have centered on White Russians. With this information in Japanese hands, the Soviets were forced to compromise on their price, as we have seen. At that stage, the Japanese were offering 100 million yen. After this, both sides made gradual concessions. The army left the negotiations entirely to the Foreign Office, with Yanagawa Heisuke, vice-minister of the army, stating, "It's disgraceful to keep haggling like this as if we were at a temple festival." Compromise was reached, with the figure of 140 million yen offered by Hirota.

The deal was concluded between Manchukuo, Japan, and the Soviet Union around a month later, on March 23, at the Official Residence of the Foreign Minister in Tokyo. Present were, among others, Foreign Minister Hirota, Vice-Foreign Minister Shigemitsu Mamoru, Ambassador Yurenev, Benedict Ignatiev Kozlovsky, and from the Manchukuo side, Ōhashi Chūichi and Sugihara Chiune.

Later, Ōhashi appraised the Soviet style of diplomatic negotiation as nonchalantly employing threats so that the opposing side gives up hope, but also making bold concessions. He wrote that the Soviets were easier to deal with than the Americans, who stuck to their basic arguments and would not concede an inch. He based this evaluation mainly on the negotiations for the Soviet-Japanese Neutrality Pact of 1941, but the Soviet turnaround in the CER negotiations probably remained strong in his memory.

Sugihara's Decision to Return to Japan

On July 1, around three months after the conclusion of the CER negotiations, Sugihara resigned from the Manchukuo Foreign Affairs Department and returned to its Japanese counterpart. When he was first transferred to Manchukuo at Ōhashi's request, it was agreed that he would be permitted to return to the Japanese Ministry if he wished to quit service in Manchukuo. However, Sugihara's sudden decision to return to Japan so soon after a success that had exceeded all expectations of those around him was, to say the least, unexpected. His second wife, Yukiko, whom he married after he returned to Japan, later spoke about the reason for his resignation: "He could not stand the way the Japanese in Manchuria treated the Chinese as if they were not human beings."[15] This clearly expresses Sugihara's humanitarian

---

15 Sugihara Yukiko, *Shinpan rokusennin no inochi no biza* [Visas for life for six thousand, new edition] (Tokyo: Taishō Shuppan, 1993), p. 34.

side. However, it seems too simple a reason for the thirty-five-year-old to have reached such a life-changing decision. There were, in fact, at least three further factors behind his resignation that he felt unable to disclose even to his wife. Perhaps the most important was that he was being compelled to run errands for the military. Shimura Giichi, a friend of Sugihara's from the Harbin period, has revealed that Colonel Hashimoto Kingorō proposed Sugihara become an army spy in exchange for a considerable raise. Sugihara himself also noted in an account written late in life that "I received a proposal concerning a large amount of operational expenses, but refused it outright."[16]

A word is perhaps necessary here concerning Hashimoto Kingorō. The army of that period was full of loose cannons, but Hashimoto was one of the wildest, involving himself in various plots. At the time of the Manchurian Incident, he worked actively as Chief of the Russian Section of the General Staff to expand its impact behind the scenes. He was also a core figure in the March and October incidents of 1931, which were coup d'état attempts to topple the party governments of the time and set up cabinets packed with hardliners within the army. These attempts were ultimately unsuccessful, but they had their sympathizers in the higher echelons of the military, and Hashimoto received only a slap on the wrist for "going too far." Thus, as early as 1934, he was appointed a Commanding Officer in the 2nd Heavy Field Artillery Regiment and promoted to colonel.

Why did Hashimoto think to use Sugihara and his intelligence network? As far as the army was concerned at the time, its greatest potential enemy was the Soviet Union. Diplomatic relations were not so straightforward as to be improved simply with the resolution of the CER purchase negotiations. Border incidents had continued to flare up during the course of the negotiations, and in fact, instead of decreasing after their conclusion, became ever more severe and frequent. It appears that the decision was made to continue to employ crack intelligence gathering teams such as Sugihara's, not to disband them. However, Sugihara was reluctant to expose his collaborators to danger, leaving him little choice but to resign from the Manchukuo Foreign Affairs Department.

---

16 Sugihara, Ketsudan: Gaikōkan no kaisō.

The second factor has to do with Sugihara's wife, Klaudia. According to Kasai Tadakazu, Sugihara's friend who, like him, came from Gifu Prefecture, the Kenpeitai (Military Police Corps) suspected Sugihara of passing Manchukuo intelligence to the Soviets through his White Russian wife. In other words, there were suspicions that he was a double agent. Sugihara was in danger of being caught in a trap into which competent intelligence officers sometimes fell. As the intelligence war intensified, those concerned with intelligence gathering were the first to be suspected if leaks occurred. It was not at all surprising that suspicion should fall on Sugihara, with his White Russian wife. We should also include here that jealousy was perhaps engendered by his success in the CER negotiations. On December 30, 1935, Sugihara and Klaudia divorced by mutual consent, but in fact they had been living apart since July, when Sugihara resigned from the Foreign Affairs Department and left Manchukuo.

The third possible factor concerns a fact recently revealed in a study by Professor Nakami Tatsuo of the Tokyo University of Foreign Studies. Just around the time Sugihara left Manchukuo's Foreign Affairs Department, there was an increase in personnel sent from Japan who had passed the examination for elite diplomats. When the Department was being set up, Ōhashi had hastily gathered its personnel together. Morishima Morito wrote mockingly of the situation, "Just like the first performance of a country play in the olden days, it was a case of first come, first served, each filling the positions they liked." Sugihara's promotion to virtually head the Russia section had been exceptional for a man of his age and would have been unthinkable in Japan itself. By around May or July 1935, however, personnel sent from Japan comprised the core of the Department, and this was the very time Sugihara resigned from it. Even if he had remained, his prospects were not necessarily bright.

Perhaps propelled by these three factors, he bid farewell to Manchuria, where he had spent more than fifteen years of his life, and returned to Japan alone.

Destabilization Operations and Intelligence

I would like to take the opportunity here to think again about the difference between destabilization operations (*bōryaku*) and intelligence activities. As we have seen, Sugihara, both during his time at the consulate-general in Harbin and at the Foreign Affairs Department in Manchukuo, was involved in a variety of intelligence activities. Some bordered on the illegal, and others were quite dangerous. However, they were essentially based on a deep personal trust, as is evident from the important information acquired by White Russian agents and the pressure it enabled the Japanese to put on the Soviets during the CER purchase negotiations.

The author Sasaki Yuzuru has observed that intelligence activities, particularly those of high quality, depend on loyalty. By contrast, destabilization operations do not need loyalty, only specific "rewards," like money. The Manchurian Incident was precisely the product of such a destabilization operation. Military actions in Manchuria, the disclosure of plans for a military coup d'état, the October Incident and other such events in Japan, and the terrorizing of the political and business communities had made it very difficult to express opinions against those of the military. Destabilization operations are actions that bend circumstances to the perpetrators' advantage using fear and violence. The usual procedure in intelligence activities, on the other hand, involves a give-and-take attitude to intelligence acquisition, based on interpersonal trust. To take information by force, of course, destroys trust and makes future activities difficult. Sasaki speculates that in Sugihara's case, he would have, on occasion, been able to gather information because of the ties of trust that he had forged, even if he could not furnish some reward.

Human intelligence (HUMINT) is a discipline of intelligence gathering that is made through interpersonal contact. For diplomats, it mainly involves the exchange of information with the foreign ministry of the country where they are stationed or with third-country diplomats. Information is exchanged between counterparts to acquire what is sought. This is the orthodox method used also by military and naval attachés.

To take the case of Sugimura Yōtarō, an exemplar of a Foreign Ministry intelligence officer to whom we will refer further below, the trust that he built up in the course of his work for the League of Nations, undertaken from a young age, proved beneficial later in acquiring intelligence. In this sense, both Sugimura and Sugihara shared an understanding of the importance of trust. In Sugihara's case, however, there is little evidence that he exchanged information at a diplomatic level. Rather, his agents were White Russians in Manchuria, and later, Poles and Jews in Lithuania and the other Baltic states. They were alike in that they were weak politically, but also in that they had a strong sense of enmity toward particular states—the White Russians to the Soviet Union and the Poles to the Soviet Union and Germany—and wanted to confound its plans. Sugihara succeeded in building ties with them based on the idea of a joint struggle. Compared with the "give-and-take" intelligence exchanges conducted by diplomats, it is easy to surmise that it was much harder to build relationships with such people.

The White Russians, like the Poles and Jews, were trapped in a situation where they had no political entity to protect them. It was only natural that they could not easily trust a third party, but Sugihara managed to win their confidence. At the heart of his skills as an intelligence officer was the ability to win the trust of the politically weak and build a sense of joint struggle with them. As such, any breakdown of trust had to be avoided at all costs, as it would result in fatal errors that could impede operations. It is said that an intelligence officer who is perceived as betraying his agents even once has no future in intelligence circles. It was all the more necessary to be careful in dealings with the politically weak, who were all the more cautious. It was of vital importance that an intelligence officer be implicitly trusted and incapable of betrayal.

Sugihara continued to pay a considerable price for his activities. As we shall see, he would be refused entry into the Soviet Union and was virtually deported from Germany. But whatever the price, he continued to protect his agents, and so people kept coming to work for him, reassured that if they worked for Sugihara, they would be safe. By leaving Manchuria as it fell prey to a flurry of destabilization operations, Sugihara was able to retain his self-respect as an intelligence officer.

CHAPTER THREE

The Enigma of the Soviet Visa Refusal

Husband and Father

When we consider the span of Sugihara Chiune's career as a diplomat, we realize he spent very little time at the Foreign Ministry in Kasumigaseki, the area of Tokyo where government offices are concentrated. As we have seen, he was appointed a consular clerk in Harbin and then spent over a decade in Manchuria, Harbin, and other places. He worked in the Ministry for only two years, from 1935 to 1937, and was then posted overseas again. It is easy to imagine that those years working in Kasumigaseki were a comparatively tranquil time for an intelligence officer like Sugihara.

The late Dr. Kurihara Ken, the eminent scholar of Japanese diplomatic history, entered the Foreign Ministry in 1935. He told me that he had caught sight of Sugihara immediately afterward, in a corridor of the Ministry. His impression of Sugihara as "a tall man who appeared very affable, with an intellectual face" was indeed suggestive of someone temporarily released from the harsh demands of being an intelligence officer. Dr. Kurihara was sent on government business to Europe early in 1941, journeying there via the Trans-Siberian Railway. He commented that he thought it curious that there should be refugees, apparently Jewish, journeying along the same line in the opposite direction, heading for Vladivostok. Dr. Kurihara recounted with clear emotion in his voice how, when he later heard about Sugihara issuing visas, he recalled the figure he had previously seen in the Ministry corridor and was able to connect it with the many frightened refugees he had noticed on the Trans-Siberian Railway.

The affability of the man in the corridor that appealed to Kurihara was not just the result of Sugihara's being temporarily relieved of the burden of intelligence work. There was likely a more personal reason. Now divorced from Klaudia, he had met Kikuchi Yukiko, the sister of a friend. This was the woman who would go on to share his life. Yukiko remembered that when they met for the first time, Sugihara wrote out his first name and asked her if she knew how to pronounce it. Despite the unusual combination of characters, she guessed the name "Chiune" correctly, delighting Sugihara. It was this little exchange that sparked his interest in her, probably in large part because she demonstrated intelligence of a kind that held great appeal for him.

They met more and more for dates, mainly in Ginza. Unlike today, that was not a period when love affairs could be conducted openly, so the sight of Sugihara nonchalantly going off to nearby Ginza on a date became the talk of the Ministry. This suggests that Sugihara, who had not lived in Japan since his late teens, was not the type of person to be overly concerned about traditional Japanese social conventions.

When he proposed to Yukiko, she asked him why he wanted to marry her. He replied, "Because I can take you to foreign countries and you won't embarrass me." There was a thirteen-year difference in their ages. Their eldest son, Hiroki, was born on September 20, 1936. At the time of Hiroki's birth, Sugihara was away on prolonged official business as an interpreter for the Japanese-Soviet negotiations in the city of Petropavlovsk, Kamchatka in the Soviet Far East over the leasing of fishing grounds then taking place there. On returning home, he had no sooner entered the house than he lifted the sleeping baby into his arms and, making no effort to disguise his pleasure, started walking around the house cooing to him, "Hey, I'm your papa."

An important turning point came at this time, not only in Sugihara's private life, but also in his work. Since his return from Manchuria, he had occupied various positions in the Section of Protocol and Personnel, the First Section of the Information Bureau, and others, but on December 26, 1936, he was notified of his transfer to the Japanese embassy in Moscow as second secretary-interpreter of the embassy. This represented a chance to finally make the most of his Russian language skills on the diplomatic stage, and he must have spent the traditional year-end and New Year break in a daze of happiness in both his public and private lives.

An Event without Precedent

On December 28, the Foreign Ministry applied through the Soviet embassy in Tokyo for a visa for Sugihara to enter the Soviet Union. However, since no visa had yet been issued by the latter half of January, the Ministry sent a telegram to the Japanese embassy in Moscow on January 22, ordering them to pressure the Soviet Foreign Commissariat. February came and still no news arrived that a visa had been issued, although Sugihara was due to leave Japan on February 6. On February 2, the Ministry again asked the Japanese embassy in Moscow to press the Soviets over the issue. Thus began an incident of a type unprecedented in Japanese-Soviet diplomatic history.

Talks began, with Sakō Shūichi, counselor at the Japanese embassy and an expert in Soviet-related fisheries issues, in charge. At first, Sakō thought that the Soviets were being cautious because Sugihara's former wife, Klaudia, was a White Russian, and he was optimistic that the problem would be easily resolved when he explained that they were already divorced. However, the Soviets did not change their attitude even after being informed of this fact.

On February 4, Benedict Kozlovsky, who in 1936 became Director of the Second Eastern Department of the Narkomindel and had for many years been involved in fisheries negotiations with Sakō, telephoned him and coldly informed him that the relevant authorities objected to Sugihara and had withheld issuing a visa. Sakō hotly protested that he knew of instances when visas had been refused to high-ranking diplomats like ambassadors and ministers, but that there was no precedent to refuse a visa to a mere embassy official like Sugihara and insisted that branding him a *persona non grata* was unreasonable. Deciding that nothing could be settled over the phone, Sakō proposed a face-to-face meeting. Kozlovsky, however, replied that the affair had already been concluded after careful deliberation by the relevant authorities, and since there existed a number of reasons for declaring Sugihara *persona non grata*, it was out of the hands of the diplomatic authorities. Claiming that a meeting was useless given this situation, Kozlovsky brushed Sakō off and hung up.

The Japanese saw this unilateral Soviet action as being "unprecedented by international convention," and heated negotiations between the two sides continued for more than a month.

The White Russian Factor

While saying there were a number of reasons for declaring Sugihara *persona non grata*, the Soviets gave no information at all about what, exactly, the problem was. Naturally enough, Sakō was not convinced, and on the day after the phone call, he visited Kozlovsky, despite his refusal to meet, demanding through personal negotiation that he take appropriate measures. Kozlovsky reiterated that the decision had been made after careful consideration by the relevant authorities and there was no room for reconsideration.

Given this, the First Section of the Bureau of European and West-Asiatic Affairs of the Foreign Ministry,[17] which dealt with the Soviet Union and neighboring countries, then discussed what measures should be taken. It stressed what Sakō had contended, that declaring *persona non grata* an ordinary embassy employee, as opposed to a head of mission, was a problem in terms of international law. Opinions were sought from two experts: Dr. Thomas Baty, a British national who worked in the Foreign Ministry as a legal adviser,[18] and Dr. Tachi Sakutarō, emeritus professor of international law at the Imperial University of Tokyo, who also worked for the Ministry. Although their views did not support the Ministry's opinion, Dr. Baty suggested that the Ministry could try retaliating. When it later did so, however, its retaliation only exacerbated the situation. Taking the views of the two experts into consideration, the Ministry abandoned the idea of objecting to the application of *persona non grata* to an individual embassy employee. Rather, they switched to a policy of continuing to take exception to the Soviets applying it unilaterally to Sugihara without making their reasons clear.

One element of the Japanese protest was the fact that Sugihara had been issued a visa the previous year to go to Petropavlovsk for the fisheries negotiations. Since the Soviets had not raised any objections to the visa application made at that time, why was there a problem now? A telegram to this effect was sent to the Japanese embassy in Moscow on February 10, ordering them to question the Russians on this point. It also stated that the Japanese

---

17 In 1934 the former European and American Bureau was divided into the Bureau of European and West-Asiatic Affairs and the Bureau of American Affairs.

18 Baty had come to Japan in 1916 as adviser to the Foreign Ministry on international law. He remained in Japan for the rest of his life. He published extensively on the subject of international law—which he saw in terms of natural law—canons regarding both theory and practice. He was thus opposed to the idea of a World Court and against internationalism. Famously, he formulated Japan's legal justification for its actions in Manchukuo. —Trans.

were prepared not to issue visas to Soviet diplomats to work in the Tokyo embassy. Despite this uncompromising stance, the Soviets still did not give their reasons for their refusal. Losing patience, the government sought to resolve the situation on February 23 by having Vice-Minister Horinouchi Kensuke call Nicolas Rayvid, the Soviet *chargé d'affaires ad interim*, to the Ministry. Now, the reason for the refusal was finally revealed: when Sugihara was at the consulate-general in Harbin, he had built close relations with White Russians who were hostile to the Soviet Union. His visa the previous year had been issued before this information had come to light. There was therefore no contradiction with the present visa refusal.

This incomprehensible Soviet response stiffened Japanese resolve, and they eventually resorted to the retaliation that Baty had suggested, refusing a visa for a Soviet diplomat appointed vice-consul at the Soviet consulate-general in Japan. Even though there was no particular problem with the appointee, it is clear from contemporary records that the deferment of the visa was intended to encourage the Soviets to reconsider their refusal of a visa for Sugihara.

Discovery of the Report on Sugihara

However, far from reconsidering, the Soviets withheld visas from four men destined for the Vladivostok consulate-general and from a diplomat appointed to the Japanese embassy in Moscow. A tit for tat was brewing, with the issue of Sugihara's visa refusal intensifying into a situation that was sabotaging the movements of diplomats to new posts in both countries.

At the same time as it was continuing its discussions with the Soviet authorities, the Foreign Ministry also interviewed Sugihara. This was the backdrop to the compilation of the 1937 Sugihara Report we have referred to already. It is found among prewar Showa-era (post-1926) Foreign Ministry documents in Section J concerning immigration and passports, in the file entitled "Foreign Laws and Regulations Regarding Passports and Visas, Incidents, and Related Dealings: The Soviet Union, Concerning Foreign Ministry Personnel." In this file can be found a variety of documents related to trouble surrounding the issuance of visas to personnel at the Japanese embassy in Moscow and at Japanese consulates and consulates-general in

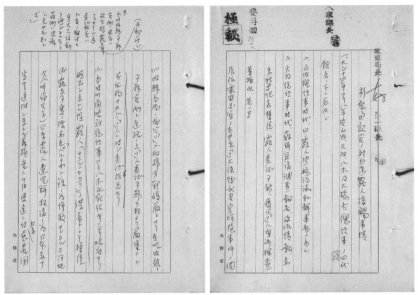

Page from the report "Concerning the Contacts with White Russians of Interpreter (Official) Sugihara." (Diplomatic Archives of the Ministry of Foreign Affairs, Japan)

Soviet territory. There is a series of documents here concerning Sugihara's visa rejection. The aforementioned record is placed between documents dated March 13 and March 17, 1937, so it was presumably filed between those dates. It was handwritten using blue ink on ten sheets of Foreign Ministry B5-sized vertical-lined paper.

There are two reasons why there is a strong possibility this report was written by Sugihara himself. First, the word *shōkan* is found in several places. This is a self-effacing expression employed by officials in writing when referring to themselves. The fact that it was used in a number of instances leaves no doubt that Sugihara is speaking in his own words. Second, Sugihara Michi, the widow of Sugihara's eldest son Hiroki, confirmed that the handwriting in the document is identical to that of the young Sugihara Chiune. This record brings to light the kind of work that Sugihara had been involved in from the time he entered the Foreign Ministry. It is extremely interesting in content, at times including Sugihara's own impressions and even his criticism of the army's high-handedness.

An Enigmatic Report, a Hidden Purpose

It was a great surprise to find, buried in this hitherto-neglected file, a document that expresses what was truly in Sugihara's mind. I cannot forget the excitement I felt when I came across this report, which had hardly been read in the more than seventy years since it was written.

However, after the initial joy at finding an important source that detailed Sugihara's early career, I realized it had a fundamental problem—the title and the content did not match. Though it purported to be about "Contacts with White Russians" as the title said, there is virtually no reference to White Russians in the report. There is only what seems like a passing mention in the final section:

> I did not have political contact with White Russians; rather my contacts were with Red Russians, in order to gather information in an intelligence sense. As a result, after my transfer to the Manchukuo Foreign Affairs Department, I found myself suspected of being a Communist.

Today it is clear that Sugihara ran his intelligence network of White Russians during the negotiations for the purchase of the CER. Was it perhaps necessary to conceal this from the Foreign Ministry at the time? This is a very important point. If during the negotiations, which had been conducted by the Japanese based on Sugihara's claims, the Soviets had produced concrete proof of Sugihara's contacts with the White Russians, it would have been a great embarrassment for Japan. Having a guilty conscience, Sugihara's safest response would have been to straightforwardly explain the circumstances behind his contacts with the White Russians, asserting that it had been necessary for the state—since, in fact, the Japanese had succeeded in drastically lowering the purchase price of the CER—and refer the decision to his superiors.

What did Sugihara intend by explicitly denying any political contact with White Russians? At the end of the report, he wrote that, after the Manchurian Incident, the White Russians tended to exaggerate their relationship with the Japanese, claiming to be old acquaintances even if they had met a person only once. Care was needed, he concluded. This can be interpreted to some extent as a conscious attempt by Sugihara to throw his superiors off the track.

Advancing a theory based on hindsight is something that should be meticulously avoided in historical research. However, considering later events, I can't help thinking that Sugihara was confident that the Soviets did not possess any concrete information regarding his intelligence activities with the White Russians. Perhaps he saw the continued Soviet attitude of bluffing their way out of difficult situations as proof that they had no firm evidence. There is every possibility, therefore, that even in an official report to the Foreign Ministry, he took it upon himself to keep his contacts with the White Russians under wraps. There was a certain "gamble" involved in this, but it was a strategy based on his experience as an intelligence officer and the confidence that experience engendered.

Shigemitsu Mamoru Steps In

Since neither the talks between Sakō and Kozlovsky nor those between Horinouchi and Rayvid brought any resolution, Shigemitsu Mamoru, the Japanese ambassador to Moscow, stepped in. As foreign minister, Shigemitsu would later be one of the signatories of the Instrument of Surrender aboard the battleship USS *Missouri*, which brought the Second World War to an end in 1945. He was a leading figure in Japanese diplomacy in the 1930s, serving as vice-foreign minister under Foreign Ministers Uchida Yasuya and Hirota Kōki. His appointment to Moscow was announced in August 1936 and he took up his post the following November. He was confronted with the Sugihara affair almost immediately.

Shigemitsu was an accomplished diplomat who confidently negotiated with the Soviets at the time of the Zhanggufeng Incident, a border conflict between Manchukuo and the Soviet Union in July–August 1938, and eventually achieved an outcome regarded as advantageous to the Japanese. He was well known as a copious

Shigemitsu Mamoru.
(Diplomatic Archives of the Ministry of Foreign Affairs, Japan)

writer, and a great many records and reports critical of the Soviet Union remain from his time at the Japanese embassy in Moscow.

He was distinctly different from the pro-Axis diplomats who were sympathetic to Germany and Italy. Following his posting to the Soviet Union, he was appointed ambassador to Great Britain in September 1938 (taking up his position a month later) and, following the outbreak of the Second World War in September 1939, he sent accurate and detailed reports back to Kasumigaseki regarding the rapidly changing situation in Europe, strongly warning of the danger of getting involved in a European war. After the war, he was tried as a "Class A" war criminal at the International Military Tribunal for the Far East (the Tokyo War Crimes Trial) at the insistence of the Russians and given a sentence of seven years' imprisonment that could be seen as their revenge for the Zhanggufeng Incident.

Let us now return to the Sugihara affair. Shigemitsu met with Boris Stomonyakov, Second Deputy Commissar of Foreign Affairs, on February 28, 1937, and declared that investigations undertaken in Japan revealed no evidence that Sugihara had had any political contacts with White Russians while he was posted in Manchukuo. Shigemitsu made a formal request that Sugihara's visa be issued and stated that as ambassador, he would take full responsibility for Sugihara's conduct as an embassy official. Stomonyakov expressed his surprise that the Japanese government was obsessed with "such a small matter" and repeated that the decision had been made based on a number of reports and that there was no room for reconsideration. Shigemitsu pointed out that Manchukuo was within Japan's sphere of influence, so it had been easy for the Japanese authorities to investigate this affair. Since this was an investigation concerning an issue in a place beyond the reach of Soviet authorities, the Soviet investigation must have been limited. In the circumstances, Japan's investigation had greater credibility. Stomonyakov refuted this in a way that defied comprehension, saying, "A daily paper published in Tianjin [Tientsin] on January 1, 1937, contained a congratulatory address to White Russians residing in Tianjin, in the names of the commander of the army of occupation in China and the [Japanese] consul-general in that city." This was a criticism of Japanese policy toward White Russians, and it goes without saying that it had absolutely nothing to do with the question of Sugihara's contacts with White Russians.

This illogical counterargument perhaps means that the Soviets had not been able to get their hands on any solid proof of Sugihara's contacts with White Russians. If they had produced any at this time, they could have caused Shigemitsu to lose face, and claim for themselves an overwhelming advantage. Their attitude of bluffing their way out of situations is itself, it seems to me, proof of the correctness of Sugihara's "reading" of the situation. There is a possibility that the intelligence activities conducted by Sugihara at the time of the CER purchase negotiations not only lowered the price of the railway significantly, but were also ingenious enough to have disguised beyond all speculation the routes by which he obtained his Soviet intelligence.

Sugihara's outstanding CER success, however, taught the Russians a lesson about the danger he posed and caused them to take action against him in the form of the unprecedented visa refusal. They clearly saw him as a menace. If they had broken Sugihara's intelligence network, they might well have permitted him to enter the country and have left him at large, but under surveillance. Something very similar happened around the same time with a Japanese diplomat named Terasaki Hidenari.

Terasaki is known in Japan as the diplomat who was the model for the father of the heroine in Yanagida Kunio's eponymous novel, *Mariko* (1980). Incidentally, it was Terasaki's patron Shigemitsu who gave Mariko her name as a baby. Terasaki was appointed first secretary at the Japanese embassy in Washington at the end of March 1941 and was actively involved in the negotiations to avert war. It is now known that the FBI had detailed knowledge of his activities from wiretapping and opening letters, but he was left at large to allow the government to find out what Japan was up to. It is classic tradecraft in the intelligence world to leave a foreign agent be if his movements can be easily followed, so that his activities can be monitored. It is the ones like Sugihara who leave no trace of their activities that are the most feared. It is hardly surprising that the Soviet Union was cautious about him.

Ambassador Shigemitsu protested that the Japanese government could not possibly accept the Soviet explanation and expressed frustration that a Foreign Ministry appointment had been rejected without adequate reason.

Stomonyakov then pointed out that permission had not been withheld from Japanese diplomats as a whole, but only from Sugihara. This revealed the Soviet Union's true motive. After this meeting ended without agreement, Counselor Sakō met with Kozlovsky on March 10 and once again complained of the unfairness of the Soviet response. The Soviets remained inflexible and the Japanese government eventually had no choice but to cancel Sugihara's posting.

I would like here to delve a little deeper into the background of this incident, extraordinary in the annals of diplomatic history, because deteriorating relations between Japan and the Soviet Union may have played a role in it. As we have seen, Sugihara was ordered to the Japanese embassy in Moscow at the end of December 1936. Just a month before, on November 25, Japan and Germany had concluded the Anti-Comintern Pact, an agreement to counter the menace of Communism. The Soviet Union regarded this agreement as an intended pincer attack by the two countries. It retaliated in a number of ways, such as refusing to sign the fisheries convention that had been approved the previous month and increasing pressure on Japan's oil and coal concessions in North Sakhalin. The refusal of a visa to Sugihara was also part of this retaliation.

The Spanish Civil War: An Unexpected Consequence

There was another factor—the Soviet Union's perception of the White Russians in Manchuria as posing a threat—that seems to have worked against Sugihara. In April 1936, the Soviets protested that the Japanese were aiding movements by White Russians in Manchukuo, an accusation which the Japanese denied as unfounded. The matter seemed to rest there, but the outbreak of the Spanish Civil War in July sparked an unexpected upsurge in political activity by Manchukuo's White Russian community.

E. H. Carr, one of the greatest British historians of the twentieth century, pointed out both the importance and the unexpectedness of the Spanish Civil War as the most significant event of 1936, in that it had broken out in a country which for a long time had played an inconsequential role in international politics. In 1936, the Spanish government was in the hands of the Popular Front, a coalition of several left-wing political groups. The previous year, the Soviet-backed Comintern (Communist International) had advocated the formation of popular fronts as a political strategy to counter the rise of Fascism, and they went on to form governments both in France and Spain (in 1936). On July 17, the military under General Francisco Franco revolted and staged a coup d'état against the Popular Front. A brutal war, sometimes called the prelude to the Second World War, was then waged for nearly three years between the Popular Front (Republicans), backed by the Soviet Union, on one hand, and the rebel troops (Nationalists) led by Franco, aided by Germany and Italy, on the other.

The attention of the world became focused on Spain. In 1940, Ernest Hemingway, who supported the Popular Front, wrote *For Whom the Bell Tolls*, concerning an American volunteer fighting for the Republicans. Pablo Picasso, a native of Spain, painted his powerful anti-war "Guernica" in 1937 in response to the indiscriminate bombing of the Basque town of Guernica by German planes fighting on behalf of Franco.

The response of the Japanese government to the Spanish Civil War was not clear-cut. Both Germany and Italy recognized Franco's government on November 18, 1936, and encouraged Japan to follow suit. However, Japan did not do so until December 1, 1937. The United States and Great Britain recognized the Nationalist government in 1939. The timing of Japan's recognition is symbolic of its complicated position, wavering between the Axis powers and the Allies of the impending Second World War.

The sympathies of large numbers of White Russians in Manchukuo lay with Franco, given their anti-Soviet sensibilities, and they tried to give aid, both economic and in spirit, to his cause. Unsurprisingly, their actions greatly offended Soviet sentiments. With this outbreak of anti-Soviet political activity by White Russians, it is not hard to imagine that the Soviets were wary of Sugihara, since they had not been able to catch him out. But his superb work had become a double-edged sword for him. It had aroused Soviet wariness, and as a result, he was unable to take up his posting at the place where he would have been able to make the most of his abilities: the Japanese embassy in Moscow.

It is all too ironic that Sugihara, who would go on to issue thousands of transit visas to save Jewish refugees, would himself suffer because a visa was not issued to him. It is easy to imagine that his own bitter visa experience came to mind when he decided to start issuing all those visas in Kaunas, Lithuania.

Meeting Sakō Shūichi Again

Sugihara's posting was finally decided on August 12, 1937. He was appointed second secretary-interpreter at the newly established Japanese legation in Finland. Because he had been refused a visa for the Soviet Union, he was unable to travel by the Trans-Siberian Railway, the normal route to get to Finland, and instead had to cross the Pacific and then the Atlantic by ship. At that time, it took ten days to travel by rail from Vladivostok to Moscow by train, and so would have taken at the most two weeks to get to Helsinki. However, Sugihara and his family had no alternative but to spend a month getting to their destination.

Anticipating the difficulties of traveling with a baby not yet one year old, Yukiko brought along her younger sister Kikuchi Setsuko to help. She accompanied the family, sharing the care of Hiroki and studying European culture as well. She remained with the Sugiharas until they eventually returned to Japan after the war.

The *chargé d'affaires ad interim* in Helsinki, Ichikawa Hikotarō, had been there for the past four years preparing for the opening of the legation. After being relieved, he returned to Japan and worked in the Cultural Work Bureau of the Foreign Ministry. He attached great importance to cultural exchange and so was a rarity in the Ministry at that time. He wrote a book called *Bunka to gaikō* (Culture and diplomacy) dealing with knowledge about foreign countries and the importance of cultural diplomacy. Here he introduced Finland as "a country of water, music, and sports" and vividly described its rich natural beauty, its wonderful music born out of its luxuriant nature, and its steady evolution as a healthy and cultural nation in the less than twenty years since it gained its independence from Russia. It was as if he were foretelling Finland's present prosperity.

Ichikawa's successor, the first minister to be appointed to Finland, was Sakō Shūichi, the man who, as counselor at the Japanese embassy in Moscow, had borne the brunt of the negotiations over Sugihara's visa. He was proficient in Russian and was known as an expert on the Soviet Union. He treated Sugihara extremely kindly, in private as well as official matters. Since he had not brought his wife to Finland, he often had the Sugiharas join him for drinks. He preferred *sake*, but apparently gave the Sugiharas a bottle of whiskey, saying he wasn't going to let them go home until they finished it. Yukiko spoke fondly of him, saying he had always been very good to them.

It is very likely that Sugihara's appointment to Helsinki was at Sakō's urging. Since Finland bordered the Soviet Union, it was an important listening post for Soviet intelligence, and Sakō may have wanted an intelligence officer close to him who had been so successful that he had been refused entry into the Soviet Union. As already noted, Sakō was proficient in Russian, and moreover was an excellent intelligence officer himself. After leaving Finland, he was appointed ambassador to Poland, a country with which Japan had very close ties, sharing intelligence about the Soviet Union. He was trusted by Polish Foreign Minister Józef Beck and received a large amount of important intelligence directly from him. It was particularly valuable at a time when the European situation was very strained on the eve of war, since Beck was the foreign minister of a country positioned between Germany and the Soviet Union. Besides sharing proficiency in Russian, Sugihara and Sakō were both skilled intelligence officers, and this must have further drawn them to each other.

Peaceful Finland, Dangerous Europe

In the roughly two years that Sugihara was in Finland, a rash of events occurred in Europe that would ultimately lead to war. Germany's annexation of Austria (*Anschluss*) in March 1938 sent a wave of anxiety around the world. It was at this time, too, that border clashes occurred between Poland and Lithuania, which I will refer to below.

The following September, Adolf Hitler demanded that Czechoslovakia cede Sudetenland, a region populated by large numbers of ethnic Germans, to Germany. This made all of Europe nervous. In an effort to return the situation to an even keel, Benito Mussolini arranged for a meeting to be held in Munich on September 29 between the leaders of Great Britain, France,

Germany, and Italy. Neither Great Britain nor France voiced opposition to Hitler's terms, and the annexation of Sudetenland by Germany was approved by the four countries the following day without any consultation with Czechoslovakia. British Prime Minister Neville Chamberlain declared that the Munich Agreement had guaranteed peace, but Hitler's ambitions did not rest with the acquisition of Sudetenland. In March 1939, Czechoslovakia was broken up and became the German Protectorate of Bohemia and Moravia. Even Chamberlain, who had maintained a policy of appeasement toward Germany, had to recognize that a limit had been reached.

Within Germany, persecution of Jews was intensifying. Particularly shocking was Kristallnacht, which took place on November 9–10, 1938. It had its origins in the assassination of a German diplomat at the German embassy in France by a young Jew two days earlier. Enraged, people damaged and destroyed large numbers of Jewish homes, businesses, and synagogues in both Germany and Austria. The name Kristallnacht (Crystal Night) comes from the glittering of the broken glass from the destroyed buildings. It is a beautiful name for such a terrible event. The German government blamed the Jews for the murder; many were arrested, and an enormous collective fine was imposed.

Public opinion in Great Britain and the United States condemned this atrocity, and President Franklin D. Roosevelt issued a statement saying that it was unbelievable that such a barbaric act could be perpetrated in the civilized world of the twentieth century.

After Kristallnacht, there was a large increase in the number of Jews, mainly German, attempting to flee abroad. Surviving reports document the Finnish government's agonizing over its response to Jewish refugees from Germany and Austria. There is a strong likelihood, therefore, that Sugihara saw Jewish refugees in the streets. There was also a sudden upsurge in Jewish refugees to Manchuria and Japan.

Amid the tensions building in Europe, Sugihara took the opportunity to learn to drive in Helsinki. This should not be understood as an activity made possible by a surplus of free time, but rather as part of his preparation for when he returned to the front line of intelligence gathering. In *Visas for Life*, Yukiko wrote that her husband engaged in intelligence gathering under the pretense of a family drive. A car provided him the mobility that is indispensable to the smooth running of intelligence activities. As we shall see in Chapter 8, Sugihara took the wheel himself when he engaged in his most remarkable activities.

Even as Germany and other European countries degenerated into turmoil, Finland remained at peace. The Sugihara family became even busier with the birth of their second son, Chiaki, on October 29, 1938. Stories survive concerning Sugihara's great love for classical music during his posting in Finland. He was lucky enough to have met the great Finnish composer Jean Sibelius, and was given a signed portrait of Sibelius and a record of *Finlandia*, the tone poem beloved by all Finns. The record was unfortunately lost during the war, but the portrait is said to still be a prized possession of the Sugihara family.

Sugimura Yōtarō, a Leading Figure in Intelligence

During his time in Finland, something happened that must have filled Sugihara with pride as an intelligence officer. Sugimura Yōtarō, one of the outstanding intelligence officers of his time, was then the Japanese ambassador in Paris, having been appointed in 1937. A telegram sent to the Foreign Ministry on March 4, 1938, contained a request that Sugihara be assigned to him. The telegram was marked "urgent." Though Sugimura is largely unknown today, his international reputation at the time was the highest of any Japanese diplomat. At 185 centimeters, he was well above average height for the time, and, instructed by the founder of judo, Kanō Jigorō of the Kōdōkan, he held a ranking of sixth *dan*. He was also an excellent swimmer. After he passed the Foreign Ministry examination in 1908, he was sent to Lyon University in France to study international law and, while there, asked permission to swim across the Strait of Dover. This was strongly opposed, however, by both the Japanese ambassador to London, Katō Takaaki, and the

Sugimura Yōtarō. (Diplomatic Archives of the Ministry of Foreign Affairs, Japan)

counselor at the embassy, Yamaza Enjirō, among others, so permission was refused, forcing him to give up the idea.

There is an interesting account that appears in "From Snowy Harbin," the article Sugihara wrote about taking the Foreign Ministry examination for language cadets. While he was waiting his turn to take the physical examination, he caught sight of a tall, well-built gentleman walking in the garden, with all the appearance of someone taking a leisurely stroll. He wondered whether it could have been "Mr. Sugimura, the skilled judo practitioner and diplomat." We don't know whether it was or not, but it is a testament to the fact that Sugimura was renowned as a sporting diplomat of great stature that even a young student like Sugihara knew of him.

Besides being a sportsman, Sugimura was a hard worker and a skilled socializer. In his memoirs, Nishi Haruhiko, who served as vice-foreign minister under Tōgō Shigenori, describes the atmosphere in the Foreign Ministry in the 1920s.[19] Nishi thought highly of Sugimura, who would arrive at the Ministry every morning before work and avidly read the French newspaper *Le Temps*. Nishi also wrote that he laughed so much his stomach hurt when Sugimura performed a traditional humorous dance exposing his belly at a party.

Sugimura's international fame grew as a result of his 1927 appointment as under secretary general of the League of Nations following the expiration of the term of office of Nitobe Inazō. He worked closely with Secretary General Eric Drummond, attaining great success resolving complicated international problems. However, he had to resign his position in 1933, when Japan withdrew from the League over its refusal to recognize Manchukuo, but he retained the trust he had built with diplomats from around the world.

As we have seen, Sugihara was tasked at this time to draft Japan's rebuttal to the Lytton Report in French, and there is a very strong possibility that Sugimura would have seen it. If his translation had been acknowledged by no less a person than Sugimura, who was fluent in French, it would have meant his own French was of the first order.

---

19 Nishi Haruhiko, *Kaisō no Nihon gaikō* [Reminiscences of Japanese diplomacy] (Tokyo: Iwanami Shoten, 1965).

In 1934, Sugimura was appointed ambassador to Italy, and his stature was such that, when serious international problems arose, diplomats of other countries, stationed in Italy, would visit the Japanese embassy to consult with him. Nagai Matsuzō, a doyen of diplomatic circles who had served as vice-foreign minister and as ambassador to Germany, assessed him as a person who well understood the complicated and ever-changing situation in Europe, even though he was from East Asia, and commended "his outstanding intelligence and judgment."

Today, there are preserved in the Diplomatic Archives of the Foreign Ministry a large number of voluminous and detailed reports from Ambassador Sugimura concerning the Spanish Civil War and the invasion of Ethiopia by Italy. The highlight is the large amount of information obtained through personal contacts that he had built up through his own charm. While officials in the Foreign Ministry valued his reports, they were perplexed by their quantity. Yosano Shigeru,[20] then working in the Second Section of the Bureau of European and West-Asiatic Affairs, commented that "the appeal of Ambassador Sugimura's reports is their volume," but went on to say that there were so many that they were difficult to file.

Why did Sugimura need Sugihara? I have not found any documents that provide any background for his request, but French foreign policy at the time may well provide hints.

France, feeling the menace posed by the rise of the National Socialists in Germany, sought to check German power through an alliance with the Soviet Union, and it actively backed the Soviet application to join the League of Nations. Japan saw the stability of the Soviet Union's position in Europe as something that simultaneously enabled it to adopt an aggressive attitude toward issues concerning Japan. Japan was also apprehensive that the Soviet Union might entice France and other European countries to begin creating a cordon encircling it.

Sugimura, Japan's greatest intelligence officer, realized that Soviet-French collaboration could be a threat to Japan, and there are a great many

---

20 Yosano Shigeru was the second son of the poets Yosano Tekkan and Yosano Akiko and the father of politician Yosano Kaoru.

surviving documents that corroborate this. It is not difficult, therefore, to imagine that Sugimura wanted as many people as possible to help with his intelligence activities. His eyes alighting on Sugihara, whose outstanding competence had resulted in him being denied entry to the Soviet Union, Sugimura might very well have thought Sugihara was the very person he needed. It would have been a matter of great pride for Sugihara to know that such a renowned intelligence officer wanted him.

The Foreign Ministry replied to Sugimura, saying that "regrettably" they could not accede to his request. Although no reason was provided, they likely thought it would be a waste to send Sugihara to a country far from the one in which he was an expert, and that he should instead remain stationed in a country that neighbored the Soviet Union, where he would be ready to act when problems arose. It is noteworthy that Sugimura appeared to put great store in Sugihara's intelligence capabilities even though he probably never had the chance to meet Sugihara directly.

It was extremely unfortunate for Japanese diplomacy that Sugimura became ill while in France and returned to Japan in January 1939. He died two months later, on March 24, at the all-too-young age of fifty-four. In recognition of his great service over many years, he was given an official Foreign Ministry funeral.

CHAPTER FOUR

To the Shores of the Baltic

Riga

Sugihara was notified of his reassignment from the legation in Finland on July 20, 1939. He was to go to Kaunas in Lithuania as vice-consul and set up a consulate there. Since there were no plans to appoint an official consul, he would be responsible for the consulate in an acting capacity. Given that there had been no Japanese consulate or legation in Lithuania before then, why had Sugihara been sent there? To answer this, we must first consider the relationships between Japan and the three Baltic states.

For Japanese, these countries, so close to Russia / the Soviet Union, are almost indistinguishable, but in fact their history, culture, and languages are very different. To take religion as an example, Lithuania is Catholic, but Latvia and Estonia are Protestant. Then, in contrast to the other two countries, Estonians are ethnically Asiatic, like the Finns and Hungarians. To actually visit these countries as a tourist is to be fascinated by their rich individuality, each different from the other.

After the First World War, the three countries became independent from Russia. Latvia and Estonia have long coastlines studded with excellent ports, many of which had been important naval bases[21] and commercial ports under Imperial Russia. The Soviet Union cast hungry eyes on these. Since the Soviet Union posed the main danger to Latvia and Estonia, out of necessity they often acted in concert on the diplomatic front. Lithuania, on the other hand, did not share a land border with the Soviet Union, nor did it possess much of a coastline, so it had been able to build comparatively good relations with the Soviets. The difficult diplomatic issues for Lithuania concerned problems with Germany over its one port, Klaipėda,

---

21 During the Russo-Japanese War, the base of the famous Baltic Fleet that fought the Japanese Navy was Libau in Latvia.

and dissension with Poland over its capital, Vilnius. I will discuss these further below.

Japan first selected Latvia as its listening post for the Soviet Union after the First World War. It is the central of the three countries, and during the interwar period, it was the largest in terms of area and population. Since Latvia was ideally situated to gather intelligence from Germany and Poland, Japan opened a legation in its capital, Riga, the "Paris of the Baltic," on September 1, 1929. At first, the ambassador to Germany concurrently held the position of minister to the legation and a *chargé d'affaires ad interim*

Letter giving the permission of President Smetona for consular activity to take place in Lithuania. (Diplomatic Archives of the Ministry of Foreign Affairs, Japan)

was sent to Latvia from the embassy in Berlin.[22] Those *chargés d'affaires* form an impressive list of Russian/Soviet experts, including Sugishita Yūjirō, with diplomatic experience at the Japanese embassy in Moscow spanning both Imperial Russia and the Soviet Union; Watanabe Rie, *chargé d'affaires* in Poland and consul-general in Vladivostok; and Shichida Motoharu, first secretary at the Japanese embassy in Moscow, who helped Sakō Shūichi with Sugihara's visa problem and was later consul-general in Vladivostok, then counselor at the Moscow embassy.

Yoshida Shigeru

One episode illustrates just how useful the consulate in Latvia was for intelligence gathering. Even more interesting is that Yoshida Shigeru was involved. He was a career diplomat who, as prime minister in the postwar

---

22 These officers head a diplomatic mission temporarily. In this case, where the legation was headed by a non-resident minister, their posting was more long-term. —Trans.

period, worked hard for Japan's independence. Following the resignation of the Okada Keisuke cabinet as a consequence of the 2-26 Incident in 1936, a new government was formed by Hirota Kōki, who had taken the Foreign Ministry examination for career officers at the same time as Yoshida, and Hirota proposed Yoshida as foreign minister. However, Yoshida's father-in-law, Makino Nobuaki, was a central figure in the pro-British/pro-American faction and had been targeted for assassination while staying in Yugawara during the 2-26 Incident, only escaping by a hair's breadth. This made Yoshida a potential problem. Sure enough, his appointment was vigorously opposed by the army on the grounds that Makino's son-in-law had no business being foreign minister, and the plan was frustrated. In recognition of Yoshida's services in helping him select various posts in the new cabinet, Hirota had him appointed ambassador to Great Britain, a plum posting.

On taking up his position in London in June 1936, and undaunted by the setback his ministerial career had suffered, Yoshida energetically devoted himself to cultivating contacts of all kinds to advance Anglo-Japanese relations. What particularly concerned him were reports that the Soviet Union was seeking rapprochement with Britain. We saw in the last chapter that Japan felt that French-Soviet rapprochement to be a danger to its own concerns and was alarmed that the same thing could be happening in Britain.

The January death of King George V had received unprecedented attention in the Soviet press. Foreign Commissar Litvinov was in London to attend the king's funeral and used the opportunity to meet leading politicians in what may be called "condolence diplomacy." Japanese diplomats based in Europe raised their voices in consternation at the closer relations between the two countries. Particularly notable was the reaction of Shiratori Toshio, minister to Sweden. He promoted Axis diplomacy during his time as ambassador to Italy between 1938 and 1940, and after the war was sentenced to life imprisonment as a Class A war criminal. As we shall see, Emperor Hirohito avoided visiting Yasukuni Shrine because both Shiratori and Matsuoka Yōsuke were enshrined there. At the end of January 1936, deeply concerned about the situation, Shiratori sent the following strongly-worded telegram: "Great Britain despairs of Japan and intends to ally with the Soviet Union. I would like the Japanese government not to be focused only on the China problem, but also take the European problem a little more into account."

The Soviet Union did not strike Yoshida as being as close to Great Britain as Shiratori and sensationalist newspaper reports in Japan suggested. His keen intuition gave him a sense of the real situation, but he wanted corroborating intelligence.

Anthony Eden's Visit to Moscow

A little explanation is perhaps necessary concerning what caused the rumor of Anglo-Soviet rapprochement to circulate. Anthony Eden, foreign secretary under Winston Churchill during the Second World War and prime minister from 1955 to 1957, had been deeply involved in foreign affairs from his youth. He was appointed Lord Privy Seal (a minister without portfolio) on New Year's Day in 1934 and was spoken of as a future foreign secretary.

In 1935, Eden became the first British dignitary to visit the Soviet Union. Instigating the visit was Hitler's announcement on March 16 that Germany would rearm, in violation of the Treaty of Versailles. The British government sent a delegation to Berlin on March 24, headed by Foreign Secretary John Simon and his long-time adviser Eden, to urge Hitler to prudence. When the German talks were being held in February, Ivan Maisky, the Soviet ambassador in London, suggested they go on to Moscow after Berlin. Though Simon had previously shown interest in visiting the Soviet Union, he was then having second thoughts. Eden could not understand Simon's attitude; he seemed to be nonchalantly throwing away the chance to speak with Stalin face to face. Early in March, the Cabinet decided that the Moscow visit should occur after Berlin, and that Eden, not Simon, should be involved. So after Eden left Berlin, he continued on to the Soviet Union, while Simon returned to London. Eden spent March 28–31 in Moscow and had constructive meetings with Joseph Stalin, Vyacheslav Molotov, and Litvinov, among others. He returned to London by way of Warsaw and Prague, where he exchanged views with the Polish and Czech foreign ministers, Józef Beck and Dr. Edvard Beneš. For Eden, then aged just thirty-seven, to confer with such leading European figures must have contributed greatly to his maturation as an architect of foreign policy.

Japan watched Eden's visit to the Soviet Union with a sense of foreboding. Following a policy of international cooperation against Communism, Japan was moving in the direction of isolating the Soviet Union while seeking to mend relations with other countries that had soured with the Manchurian Incident. As such, Eden's Moscow visit would have been a matter of great concern for Japan, particularly the question of whether the Far East situation had been discussed and the possibility that the Soviets had requested British cooperation in restraining Japan. Japan's Europe-based diplomats accordingly set about feverishly gathering intelligence, with Sakō Shūichi, then acting ambassador in Moscow in the absence of Ōta Tamekichi, leading these efforts. At a party held by Litvinov, Sakō had asked Eden directly whether the Far East had been discussed, but Eden denied that it had. This answer was only half true. British and Soviet documents reveal that the Soviets did bring up the Far East situation a number of times, pressing for cooperation between the two countries to restrain Japanese expansion, but Eden kept skillfully evading any definite promises.

Britain was not unmindful of Japan's concern about the visit. On March 27, the day before Eden went to Moscow, Sir Warren Fisher, permanent secretary to the Treasury, took the trouble of visiting the Japanese ambassador, Matsudaira Tsuneo. Fisher was a central figure in the faction in British political circles that was sympathetic to Japan at the time, and he explained to Matsudaira that Eden's visit was purely one of courtesy and not in the least political. There is no doubt that, until Britain let its relationship with Japan deteriorate, the British had no intention of improving relations with the Soviet Union. All the same, Japanese diplomats in Europe continued to feel uneasy as intelligence accumulated about closer relations between the two countries, evidenced, for example, by the Congress of Peace and Friendship with the U.S.S.R. held in London later that year.

Relevant Latvian Intelligence

Yoshida, who did not immediately believe reports about Anglo-Soviet rapprochement, spoke with the *chargé d'affaires* in Latvia, Sakuma Shin. Upon receiving a telegram from Yoshida seeking confirmation, Sakuma replied emphatically: "The Soviet Union fears a pincer movement from Germany and Japan and so is actively seeking a closer relationship with Great Britain. There is, however, not much possibility that they will join hands, given that their systems are so different. Also, newspapers in various European countries do not accept reports coming out of the Soviet Union without question and are extremely careful how they deal with them. Japanese newspapers, on the other hand, tend to easily believe any original reports spread by the Soviet Union, and so caution is necessary."

Referring to Sakuma's views, Yoshida reported that no factual basis could be found regarding a particularly close relationship between the Soviet Union and Great Britain. His intuition was corroborated by the intelligence from Latvia. At the time of negotiations over an anti-Comintern pact between Japan and Germany the following year, Yoshida frequently communicated his views to Kasumigaseki that Germany was an untrustworthy country and that it was Japan's relationship with Britain that was of the greatest importance. Yoshida had clearly not allowed Nazi propaganda to affect his good judgment.

Yoshida's close friend Kurusu Saburō, Japan's ambassador in Belgium, also lent support to Yoshida's opinion by sending the Foreign Ministry a stream of telegrams expressing his own opposition to an anti-Comintern pact. As we shall see later, he too was an excellent intelligence officer, and set great store on Sugihara's capabilities.

Japan, however, went ahead and signed the Anti-Comintern Pact with Germany on November 25, 1936. Yoshida and Kurusu both perceived that Japan had joined hands with Germany as a result of overestimating the severity of the Soviet threat and adhering to its own ethos of anti-Communism, thereby making its future all the more dangerous. History proved them to be right, further proving the relevance of intelligence from Latvia at the time.

The Foreign Ministry versus the Finance Ministry

The Riga legation was only supposed to be a temporary affair, staffed by a *chargé d'affaires*, so there were obvious limits to its authority. However, from around the time of the Manchurian Incident, the Foreign Ministry moved to have it upgraded to an official legation. If the *chargé d'affaires* were promoted to minister, that minister could be concurrently responsible for all the Baltic states, including Estonia and Lithuania. There was also support in Estonian government circles for this.

In 1931, Japan was one of four permanent members of the Council of the League of Nations, with much more influence internationally than it has now. Since its neighbor Latvia had an envoy in the form of a *chargé d'affaires*, Estonia wanted a Japanese diplomatic presence as well. The matter was studied principally by the First Section of the European and American Bureau at the Foreign Ministry, to the extent that a proposal was drafted for the Cabinet to give official status to the Latvian legation. However, with Japan still embroiled in the repercussions of the Manchurian Incident, it was not submitted. Japan's subsequent withdrawal from the League of Nations in 1933, in the aftermath of the Incident, marked a great turning point for its diplomacy. This left a great many scars, but perhaps the greatest concern for Japan was the loss of the League as a locus for intelligence gathering.

The latter part of the 1920s is regarded as a time when League of Nations diplomacy was at its height. The League was founded in 1920, having been established by Part One of the Treaty of Versailles. Germany, on which the Treaty had imposed astronomical amounts of reparations, was not permitted to be a member and was placed under strict surveillance. The turning point for Germany came with the Locarno Treaties of 1925. Germany pledged not to violate its western borders and, if it broke the agreement, it would be sanctioned not only by the injured country but by all the signatories of the treaties, and conversely, if Germany were invaded, the transgressor would likewise be sanctioned by all. Britain and Italy, which did not share borders with Germany, acted as guarantors. The treaties permitted Germany to become a permanent member of the Council of Nations, enhancing the activities of the League. An annual League Assembly for representatives of all member states was held each autumn at the League headquarters in Geneva. With prime ministers and foreign ministers from all the European countries attending,[23] it was a particularly important event both for making social contacts and for intelligence gathering. Having excluded itself from the League,

---

23 Japan did not send such high-ranking representatives to the League because of the distance, among other reasons.

it was all the more important for Japan to strengthen its contacts with those countries with whom it had previously cooperated in intelligence activities.

This, together with Japan's worsening relations with the Soviet Union, made Estonia, itself under Soviet threat, a very important country with which Japan might build a cooperative relationship. Estonia also wooed Japan. Negotiations over a trade agreement between the two had commenced several years previously but had broken down due to the considerable disparity between the demands of the two sides. In 1934, Estonia proposed they be reopened and, on June 21 that year, the talks bore fruit in the form of a tentative agreement, thereby bringing Estonia and Japan one step closer to each other. Estonia also placed military intelligence regarding the Soviet Union at Japan's disposal, and gave permission for the Japanese army to send officers assigned to diplomatic delegations without accreditation as military attachés to its capital, Tallinn. According to Sakuma, *chargé d'affaires* in Latvia, the intelligence from the Estonian military was more valuable than that received from Latvia and Lithuania.

This cooperative diplomatic and military relationship between the two countries was almost immediately plunged into a crisis. The cause was Japan's June 1934 dispatch of a military attaché to the legation in Helsinki. As a glance at any map of modern Europe shows, Estonia and Finland are just a stone's throw away from each other across the Baltic Sea—so close that tourists today travel by ferry to Tallinn on day trips from Helsinki. Estonia was put out that Finland had warranted an attaché while it had only an officer assigned to diplomatic delegations without accreditation as a military attaché, and it hinted it might discontinue its favorable treatment of Japan, given that it could not extend special favors to the resident officer of a country that did not dispatch a minister or a military attaché.

This problem grew to involve the Japanese army, and the General Staff in particular. The Foreign Ministry could not ignore this Estonia-related issue either, and later that year submitted a budget request to the Finance Ministry to upgrade the *chargé d'affaires* in Riga to minister, with concurrent responsibility over Estonia and Lithuania. This was refused; not only was it allocated no funds at first consideration, but it also failed to win any piece of the budget pie set aside for reconsidering and restoring initially rejected requests.

All the same, intelligence cooperation with Estonia did strengthen in the field, both militarily and diplomatically. As previously mentioned, when Anthony Eden visited the Soviet Union in 1935, Sakō Shūichi, the *chargé d'affaires ad interim* to Moscow, received a great deal of intelligence, particularly from the Estonian minister in the Soviet Union. Sakō wrote in a telegram that the Estonian minister was the person he most trusted.

In Japan, during a speech entitled "On the Improvement of Our Diplomatic Corps," delivered to the Society for Japanese Foreign Policy on March 22, 1935, Shigemitsu Mamoru distributed a handout entitled "General Principles for an Ideal Finance Ministry Budget" that mentioned sending a full-time minister to Latvia.

Itō Nobumi, minister at the legation in Warsaw who had previously been in charge of the trade agreement negotiations with Estonia, was also enthusiastic about having closer relations with Estonia. Itō had been deputy director of the Imperial Japanese Bureau for the League of Nations until Japan's withdrawal, and like Sugimura Yōtarō, was well versed in European affairs. Following the sudden death of Kawai Hiroyuki, minister to Poland, in Warsaw on August 15, 1933, he served as minister there from December 22, 1933, to July 21, 1937. His intelligence activities during the period following Japan's withdrawal from the League of Nations, when it was increasingly difficult to gain access to information, are worthy of special note.

Colonel Józef Beck served as Polish foreign minister from 1932 to 1939, until Poland was partitioned on the outbreak of the Second World War. Though he was notorious for his dislike of meeting face-to-face with foreign ambassadors and ministers, the one diplomat he would frequently meet personally was Itō. As a result, Itō often succeeded in acquiring valuable intelligence. He had realized early on the importance of intelligence about the Soviet Union. In 1934, he was concerned about the amount of anti-Japanese propaganda being disseminated in Poland by the Soviet news agency, Tass, and told Kasumigaseki that, in his opinion, countermeasures should be taken. Regarding the Estonian question, he asserted that a legation in Tallinn could take advantage of the intelligence gathering opportunities afforded by the large number of Soviet visitors to the city. He observed that Soviet citizens tended to be close-mouthed in their own country because of strict surveillance by the GPU (State Political Directorate), the intelligence service, and secret police, but when abroad, they were more loose-tongued and let information slip comparatively easily. Also, Tallinn was geographically close to Leningrad (St. Petersburg). The capital had been shifted to Moscow, but Leningrad remained one of the Soviet Union's principal cities. If the need arose to orchestrate anti-Soviet political operations, Tallinn's proximity was a plus. He stressed, therefore, the urgency of opening a legation there, going so far as to suggest that, if this would be difficult because of budgetary considerations, the legation in Poland could serve Estonia concurrently. That Itō made such a suggestion despite Poland's location south of the Baltic countries and distance from Estonia is indicative of the importance he placed on establishing a legation in Tallinn.

Onodera Makoto and the Foreign Ministry

With the appointment of Major Onodera Makoto as military attaché to the Latvian legation, the army's demands heightened. Born in 1897—three years Sugihara's senior—Onodera was one of the army's best intelligence officers and, as such, would have a close connection with Sugihara. He had graduated from the Imperial Military Academy in 1919, the same year Sugihara took the Foreign Ministry examination for language cadets, and in 1925, the year after Sugihara entered the Foreign Ministry, he had entered the Army War College, graduating three years later. After the Manchurian Incident, he worked for the Russia and China Department of the General Staff, gathering Soviet- and China-related intelligence. This experience grounded him in intelligence, which played a part in his appointment as military attaché in 1935, a position he took up in early January 1936.

Building trust and sharing information with local military counterparts were essential to the intelligence gathering work of a military attaché. Not only did Onodera establish connections with the Latvian military, but he also steadily built up an intelligence network among the military attachés from other countries based in Latvia and developed a reputation for providing reliable information. Of all the foreign attachés, he had a particularly close personal relationship with the Estonian, Colonel Villem Saarsen, and was keenly aware of the excellence of the Soviet intelligence Estonia provided, both in quantity and quality. Thus motivated to build a closer cooperative relationship with the Estonian military, he communicated to the General Staff his wish to combine his position with that of military attaché to Estonia and Lithuania.

On July 10, 1936, the Foreign Ministry sent a communication to the Finance Ministry entitled "Significant National Policy Associated with the Foreign Ministry Budget of 1937." An important topic it discussed was the establishment and enhancement of embassies and legations in the Soviet Union and the countries on its periphery, with emphasis on the enhancement of the Latvian legation. At this time, too, securing a budget proved difficult, and the Foreign Ministry, running out of patience, accordingly upgraded the Latvian *chargé d'affaires* to minister on its own authority, simultaneously making it a position that applied concurrently to Estonia and Lithuania. On December 23, 1936, Sakuma Shin was appointed, with cabinet approval, envoy extraordinary and minister plenipotentiary. By the following year, Estonia and Lithuania had approved the proposal to allow the minister to Latvia to hold the positions of minister to Estonia and Lithuania concurrently, as a result of which the military attaché of the legation was also recognized as concurrently serving in those two countries.

If the Foreign Ministry was able to take such measures, why did it wait so many years for budget approval by the Finance Ministry? Was the Foreign Ministry emulating the example where the Japanese ambassador in Germany was concurrently minister to Latvia and a legation was established there under a *chargé d'affaires*? It doubtless intended to set up legations in Estonia and Lithuania as well, and staff them with *chargés d'affaires* and a number of legation staff. However, despite frequent requests, the Finance Ministry did not approve the budget, and as a result, the Foreign Ministry had to do the best it could within its budgetary limits. There was clearly little awareness in Japan of the importance of the Baltic states as bastions against Japan's international isolation and as bases to gather intelligence about the Soviet Union. In any case, the desperate measure paid off, and Japan's ability to access Soviet intelligence took a giant leap forward.

Once a route had been established, with Onodera periodically visiting the Estonian General Staff at Saarsen's invitation, his reports became more and more substantial. So close was the friendship between the two men that, according to the memoirs of his wife Yuriko,[24] who had accompanied him to Latvia, she and her husband spent a week touring Estonia by car with other military attachés, guided by Saarsen. She writes of being struck by the apparent material affluence of the rural villages and the happy demeanor of their inhabitants. She noted that Latvia was also, thanks to the good government of its president Kārlis Ulmanis, one of the most advanced countries in Europe in terms of the availability of meat and dairy products. She was clearly deeply impressed by the efforts of the people of the Baltic states to build their prosperity after gaining independence.

Onodera's efforts as an individual played a substantial part in restoring a relationship on the brink of collapse, and then in building an even closer one, but the sustained efforts of the Foreign Ministry as an organization were also central to this success.

The Nomonhan Incident

Let us look at the background for Sugihara's appointment to Kaunas in July 1939. Previous research has not been able to furnish a convincing reason why, after refusing Ambassador Sugimura's request to have Sugihara transferred to Paris the previous year, the Foreign Ministry was now sending him to Lithuania. A striking new explanation has recently been offered by Watanabe Katsumasa, who has studied Sugihara Chiune. Watanabe pointed out that we lose sight of the situation as a whole if we focus on Sugihara alone. There were, in fact, four other Foreign Ministry diplomats who received transfer orders on July 20, the same day as Sugihara. All five were specialists in Russian intelligence and were sent variously to the Soviet Union, Poland, and the Baltic states.

Japanese-Soviet relations at that time were greatly affected by the Nomonhan Incident the previous May. Because the border between

---

24 Onodera Yuriko, *Baruto-kai no hotori nite: Bukan no tsuma no Daitōa sensō* [On the shores of the Baltic: The Greater East Asia War of a military attaché's wife] (Tokyo: K.K. Kyodo News, 1985).

Manchukuo, the Soviet Union, and Mongolia was ill-defined, there were frequent border clashes. The gravest of these took place near the village of Nomonhan on the border between Mongolia and Manchukuo. There are still many gaps in our knowledge about the battles that took place there, but it is undisputed that the Japanese artillery was far inferior to the Soviets'. The tragic scene of battle was described by a witness, a young diplomat who experienced the fighting as a junior officer. After the war, Yagi Masao served as ambassador to Hungary (1967) and Indonesia (1969), and in his later years recorded his experiences for the Diplomatic Archives. He had passed the Foreign Ministry examination for career diplomats in 1935 and entered the Ministry in April the following year. In January 1937, he was called up and was obliged to spend the next three and a half years in the army, and it was under these circumstances that he participated in the battle of Nomonhan.

At that time, ground warfare took the form of the artillery protecting the infantry. The standard of the Soviet ordnance was equal to that of any advanced nation, while the ordnance of the Japanese army was inferior both in caliber and quantity. The Japanese artillery regiment was almost immediately destroyed by enemy bombardment, but the infantry, thinking they were protected, kept advancing, leaving themselves exposed on the grassy plains. Large numbers were killed, mowed down by Soviet tanks. Yagi described days filled with pent-up anger and lost hope, seeing his men wounded and killed.

The inadequacy of the army's ordnance reached the emperor's ears. He was disappointed that the army had learned nothing from its experience at Zhanggufeng the previous year, where it was clear that Soviet artillery was superior. Even the emperor had heard that the army had failed to learn from its past military encounters with the same opponent; this points to the seriousness of the problems it faced.

At a loss as to how to resolve the situation, Itagaki Seishirō, the army minister, asked Foreign Minister Arita Hachirō at a meeting of the five core ministers of government[25] on July 17 to resolve the issue by diplomatic means. However, no matter how much the army leadership wanted a cease-fire, the field army stubbornly continued fighting, and the casualties grew. The Foreign Ministry pressed on regardless, seeking a resolution through diplomatic negotiations as Itagaki had asked. Because this meant the need for Soviet intelligence was even greater than before, five trained experts in Soviet issues were posted to countries bordering the Soviet Union. One of these was Sugihara.

The double-headed eagle, the coat of arms of the Romanov dynasty, appears designed to look out over both Europe and Asia. We must not lose sight of the fact that the Soviet Union is a vast country spanning both continents. Watanabe Katsumasa hit the nail on the head when he linked Japanese diplomatic measures in Europe with the border conflicts in the Far East.

The Five Experts

An examination of the five men dispatched at this time reveals a number of very interesting points. Though it is a little involved, let us take a closer look at them (except Sugihara) in terms of their names, careers, postings, and ranks on July 20.

Shimada Shigeru studied Russian at the Tokyo School of Foreign Languages. After graduation, he passed the *shokisei* examination and entered the Foreign Ministry in 1907. He worked all over Russia both before and after the revolution and, starting in 1932, was secretary (*shokikan*) at the Japanese embassy in Moscow. He was appointed first secretary at the legation in Latvia (with concurrent responsibility for Estonia and Lithuania) on July 20, 1939, and frequently traveled to Tallinn to set up a diplomatic office there, where he was posted after it opened.

Ōta Hideo was born in 1896 and studied business and diplomatic English at Keio University in Tokyo. He passed the Foreign Ministry examination for language cadets a year before Sugihara and studied Russian in

---

25 *Goshō kaigi* (Five Ministers' Conference) were meetings of the prime minister, foreign minister, finance minister, and the ministers of the army and navy. Instituted in 1933, it was Japan's highest decision-making body regarding national policy. —Trans.

Khabarovsk, Vladivostok, and other places. He entered the Foreign Ministry in 1922 as a *shokisei*. He was posted in various places in the Soviet Far East and Manchuria, including Nikolayevsk and Harbin (overlapping Sugihara's tenure) and at the Japanese embassy in Moscow in 1929. He subsequently served as vice-consul in Novosibirsk, and then returned to the embassy in Moscow. On July 20, 1939, he was posted to Latvia (with joint responsibility for Estonia and Lithuania) as third secretary at the legation.

Honda Ryūhei, born in 1896, studied Russian at the Tokyo School of Foreign Languages, and in 1922 entered the Foreign Ministry as a *shokisei*, serving concurrently with the Japanese Expeditionary Army in North Sakhalin until 1925.[26] After working in Khabarovsk and then in the Second Section of the Foreign Ministry's Bureau of Commercial Affairs, he was posted to the Japanese embassy in Moscow in 1932. Starting in 1934, he worked in Manchuria and in Soviet territory in the Far East. On July 20, 1939, he was appointed first-class interpreter at the embassy in Moscow.

Gotō Yasutsugu was born in 1898 and, after graduating in Russian from the Tokyo School of Foreign Languages, worked as an interpreter at the Russian embassy in Tokyo. In 1921, he became a student interpreter in the Foreign Ministry and worked in the Far East. In 1925, the year of the Soviet-Japanese Basic Convention, he was posted to Odessa, giving him experience of working not only in the Far East but also in the European part of the Soviet Union. He later worked in the Second Section of the Foreign Ministry's Bureau of Commercial Affairs and again in various parts of the Far East. He was posted to the legation in Poland in 1937. On July 20, 1939, he was dispatched as vice-consul to Lviv (Polish: *Lwów*; Russian: *Lvov*) in eastern Poland (now Ukraine).

All five men shared the same attributes of being noncareer officers and Russian specialists in the Foreign Ministry. The commitment shown by the

---

26 In 1919, Northern Sakhalin, with its valuable oil reserves, was under the control of the Kolchak government in Omsk. After Kolchak's execution in February 1920, Bolsheviks seized Alexandrovsk, and Japanese troops were sent to protect Japanese personnel and interests there. The Bolsheviks fled and Japan took control of North Sakhalin. The Japanese Expeditionary Army for Sakhalin was set up in August 1920 with its headquarters at Alexandrovsk. It left northern Sakhalin in May 1925, following the Soviet-Japanese Basic Convention that had been signed that January. —Trans.

Ministry at that time to train professionals in Russian intelligence, as well as the deployment of these five experts at the same time, shows the degree to which Foreign Minister Arita and the Ministry as a whole devoted themselves to finding a solution to the Nomonhan Incident.

Sugihara's career up to then somewhat paled in comparison to those of the other four. He was the youngest of the group, and three of the others had entered the Ministry after graduating in Russian at the Tokyo School of Foreign Languages. The odd man out here was Ōta. He too had studied Russian as a foreign language cadet, and in this sense resembled Sugihara, but he differed in terms of the length of time he had worked at the Japanese embassy in Moscow. Both Shimada and Honda had also worked there, and even if Gotō had not worked in Moscow, he had European experience through his posting to Odessa. On the other hand, Sugihara, having had his visa refused, had no experience working in European Russia. Why, then, was he included in this hand-picked group of experts?

Why Kaunas?

A hint to answer this question can be found in Kaunas, his new post. As we have seen, both the Foreign Ministry and the General Staff had an active working relationship with Estonia over Soviet intelligence. Lithuania, on the other hand, was not regarded as a potential partner. It did not share a border with the Soviet Union and there were no unresolved issues outstanding between the two countries. The main purpose in bringing Estonia and Lithuania under the control of the Latvian legation in 1937 had been to strengthen ties with Estonia to secure Soviet intelligence. In contrast, there was no urgent reason for Japan to upgrade its diplomatic status with Lithuania at this stage; the only possible reason would perhaps be to facilitate smooth negotiations in the event that Lithuania's relations with Poland and Germany worsened as a result of territorial disputes. It was, in fact, rather an act of courtesy: to leave Lithuania out would risk hurting that country's feelings.

After the First World War, Japan, a permanent member of the Council of the League of Nations, acted as a guarantor to a large number of treaties concerning complicated European border issues. This meant that it could

The Kaunas consulate (Sugihara House).

not remain indifferent to Lithuania's territorial disputes with Germany over the Klaipėda (German: *Memel*) territory and with Poland over its annexation of Vilnius (Polish: *Wilno*; German: *Wilna*), Lithuania's historic capital. However, by the time of the reassignment of Sugihara and the others in July 1939, both issues had been settled, though not to Lithuania's satisfaction.

In 1920, Poland was effectively in control of Vilnius, a significant number of whose inhabitants were Poles, even though the League of Nations had placed it under Lithuanian control. Diplomatic relations between the two countries were severed over the Vilnius issue. Then, on March 11, 1938, a Polish border guard crossed the frontier and was shot by a Lithuanian soldier. This incident flared into a major crisis. Poland demanded that Lithuania immediately restore diplomatic relations and renounce all claims to Vilnius. Lithuania hoped that the League of Nations, or a major power like Great Britain or France, might intervene. However, with the *Anschluss* on March 13, the eyes of the world were turned far from the Baltic, and no country responded to Lithuania's appeal, giving it no choice but to capitulate. With Vilnius under Polish control, Kaunas was the provisional capital of Lithuania throughout the interwar period. The city is still dotted with memorials to peace and Lithuanian independence that were erected at that time.

Before the First World War, the port of Klaipėda and the Klaipėda region belonged to Germany. In 1924, the League of Nations recognized Klaipėda as Lithuanian territory, but in the 1930s, it became one of the foci of German demands for the return of its former lands. Lithuanian Foreign Minister Juozas Urbšys made a brief stopover in Germany on his way back from attending the coronation of Pope Pius XII on March 12, 1939, and the question of Klaipėda was taken up when he met with German Foreign Minister Joachim von Ribbentrop. The latter stated that security in the region had worsened, and that it was probably only a matter of time before the blood of ethnic Germans there would be spilled. If this should happen, he threatened, there would be an immediate response by the German army. There was only one road open to Lithuania: to cede Klaipėda to Germany. Urbšys returned home and discussed the matter with the government. Knowing it could not resist Germany, Lithuania signed a treaty to that effect on March 22. Urbšys met with Hitler in Berlin in May that year. Hitler reiterated that Germany wanted peace above all things and was doing everything it could to maintain friendly relations with its neighbors. Turning to Klaipėda, he stated that it had been regrettably abandoned as a result of the Great War, but now that Germany had regained its place as a great nation, it could not let the matter rest.

With the settling of the territorial claims made on Lithuania, it is unlikely that the Foreign Ministry would have opened a consulate in Kaunas solely to enable it to better respond to territorial disputes. Kaunas was, however, Lithuania's provisional capital, and even if it had little importance as a place to gather Soviet intelligence, Japan had to send someone as an act of courtesy. As such, the Foreign Ministry had to decide who could be spared for this post. Shimada, the eldest of the group and the one with the most experience, was sent to the all-important Estonia. Sugihara, on the other hand, was the youngest, and while his competency was an unknown quantity, he had shown promise as an officer responsible for gathering Soviet intelligence. It is possible, therefore, that he was sent to Kaunas so that he could be dispatched to support other diplomats if problems in the area surrounding the Soviet Union became more serious and, in the meantime, gain further experience in intelligence gathering.

Fate is an ironic thing. Of the five experts sent to this sensitive region, Sugihara, posted to a place that seemingly posed the fewest problems, would later find his location in Kaunas forced him to grapple with an extraordinarily thorny issue.

CHAPTER FIVE

The Lithuanian Intelligence Network

The Rhetoric of Defense against Communism

There can be no argument that Nazi Germany was a negative presence rarely seen before in human history, one that brought boundless tragedy to the world. One of its professed policies was anti-Communism. It was, in part, this common goal of fighting Communism that unfortunately prompted Japan to join hands with Germany.

As far as can be ascertained from extant Foreign Ministry records, the subject of anti-Communism first arose between the two countries on April 18, 1934, when the Japanese ambassador to Berlin, Nagai Matsuzō, met with German Foreign Minister Konstantin von Neurath. Neurath was critical of Japan's treatment of Germany in the First World War. In his view, neither country had vested interests to such a degree that they should resort to war but, nevertheless, Japan had joined the Allies and attacked Germany. Nagai replied to this rebuke by saying that whatever the problems of the past, recent relations between the two countries were improving. Neurath's attitude softened, and he suggested that this was because the establishment of Hitler's cabinet brought the guiding spirit of Germany close to Japan's. When Nagai observed that Japan was a bulwark against the menace of Bolshevism in the east as Germany was in the west, Neurath agreed.

Air Traffic Minister Hermann Göring said the same thing on May 7 that year. Göring had been a member of the Nazi Party from the start, joining in 1922, and was very close to Hitler. Göring would later be sentenced to death at the Nuremberg Trials. Invited to a party hosted by Nagai, he stated that he wanted to speak with him alone. Moving to a separate room, Göring insisted that, as Germany was striving to be a bastion against Bolshevism in Europe, so Japan should be in Asia.

In his Confidential Memo on Autarky (August 1936) in which he drew attention to the need to prepare for war in four years, Hitler stated: "Apart from Germany and Italy, only Japan can be regarded as a Power standing firm in the face of the world peril of Bolshevism,"[27] singling out Japan as one of the very few countries with which Germany could share its aversion to Communism.

The increase of Soviet pressure on Japan by building better relations in Europe to secure its western borders was perceived by Japan as a threat. As we have seen, Japan was overly concerned about Soviet intentions toward France and Great Britain in this respect. Germany and Japan saw their interests as being in agreement and jointly signed the Anti-Comintern Pact on November 25, 1936, with Italy joining them the following year.

From the summer of 1938, Germany started negotiations to expand the pact into a military alliance against their hypothetical enemies: the Soviet Union, Great Britain, and France. The cabinet of Hiranuma Kiichirō, which was formed in January 1939, continued discussions over the question of a tripartite alliance, holding more than sixty meetings of the Five Ministers' Conference. Only Army Minister Itagaki Seishirō was in favor of a military alliance; the other four ministers were opposed. Though Foreign Minister Arita Hachirō had also been foreign minister in 1936 when the Anti-Comintern Pact was signed, he was absolutely opposed to a military alliance that treated Britain and France as enemies. This stance drew the ire of young army officers, who told him that, if he approved the alliance, he would become prime minister, but if he continued to oppose it, he was a dead man.

German-Soviet Nonaggression Pact

News of the signing of the German-Soviet Nonaggression Pact (Ribbentrop-Molotov Treaty) on August 23, 1939, sent shockwaves, not only in Japan, but around the world. Let us look at a few excerpts of telegrams sent from Japanese missions regarding the dismay of other countries as reported in their respective newspapers:

---

27 "Unsigned Memorandum" (August 1936). In *Documents on German Foreign Policy: From the Archives of the German Foreign Ministry*. Washington, D.C.: United States Government Printing Office, 1957–1964. Series C (1933–1937), The Third Reich: First Phase, Volume 5: 5 March–31 October, 1936. Document Number 490, pp. 853–62. (English translation accredited to U.S. Department of State Division of Language Services)

"The news of the conclusion of the German-Soviet Nonaggression Pact came like a bolt out of the blue." (Ambassador Shigemitsu, London)

"A great turning point that has the gravest results for the general situation in Europe." (Ambassador Horinouchi Kensuke, Washington)

"The desire for a war among nations has been a long-held policy of the Soviet Union. It is a mistake to cherish hopes about the Soviet Union." (Miyazaki Katsutarō, *chargé d'affaires ad interim*, Paris)

"The conclusion of this pact, in short, is a capitulation by Germany in recognition of Soviet force." (Ambassador Kurusu, Brussels)

"Astounded at first—had the Soviets gone mad, was it an April Fool's trick by them?" (Ōtaka Shōjirō, minister to Latvia)

After the first shock, the newspapers recovered their calm and began analyzing the consequences of the signing. Two countries were predictably left at a disadvantage by the pact. The first was Poland, which would end up being partitioned between Germany and the Soviet Union, and the second was none other than Japan. At the time, Japan was heavily involved in war with China and wanted somehow or other to prevent other countries from coming to China's aid. The Sino-Soviet Nonaggression Pact had been signed between the Republic of China and the Soviet Union in Nanjing on August 21, 1937, which meant China and the Soviet Union were on friendly terms. By signing the pact with Germany, the Soviets were able to relieve themselves of causes of concern in the west and Japan feared they would then strengthen their aid to China. It was widely trumpeted in China that Japan had been stabbed in the back by its friend Germany and now stood alone.

There were wide repercussions in Japan. On August 23, the same day as the signing, both army and navy ministers agreed that Japan's policy toward Europe needed to be rethought from the ground up. On the 25th, the cabinet made the official decision to discontinue negotiations over a tripartite alliance, and on the 28th, the cabinet resigned, with Prime Minister Hiranuma declaring that the situation in Europe was complex and mysterious. The Nonaggression Pact had an impact on many countries, but Japan was the only one to experience the wholesale resignation of its cabinet.

Foreign Minister Arita voiced objections to Hiranuma's declaration and the cabinet's resignation. "This declaration is problematic for me as foreign minister.

It was precisely because we came to oppose a tripartite alliance that Germany showed its true colors and revealed itself to be unworthy of trust. I do not think that this is a failure of diplomacy. As such, I cannot agree to the cabinet's resignation for reasons of diplomacy." However, Hiranuma did not change his mind.

The Sugihara Family Arrives in Kaunas

Sugihara Chiune and his family arrived at Kaunas Station on August 28. He must have received news of the German-Soviet Nonaggression Pact somewhere between Helsinki, which he left on August 25, and Kaunas. That same day, the cabinet resigned in Japan. It was uncanny timing, with upheavals both international and domestic.

It must have been clear to Sugihara that Lithuania's neighbor Poland was in a precarious position, like a candle in the wind. The Japanese ambassador in Warsaw at that time was Sakō Shūichi, Sugihara's old superior who had entrusted him with important matters both public and private. Sakō had not been accompanied by his wife while he was in Helsinki, but she had joined him in Warsaw—a matter of concern given that the city was now facing an impending crisis. As such, Sugihara had much to worry about as soon as he arrived in Kaunas, notably the safety of Sakō and his wife and the direction in which Japanese diplomacy was heading.

In Japan, there was a race to select a new prime minister following the collapse of the Hiranuma cabinet. Among the names that came up were Konoe Fumimaro, Hirota Kōki, and General Ugaki Kazushige, but all three were removed from contention, either because they declined or because their candidacy was strongly opposed. Finally, the choice fell on General Abe Nobuyuki, perceived as a "safe" candidate. His foreign minister was not chosen from the ranks of diplomats. The appointment of Admiral Nomura Kichisaburō, who had a number of British and American contacts, to this position because of the priority Japan put on relations with the United States was, I think, an error in Japanese diplomacy. According to the daily *Tokyo Asahi Shimbun* at the time, the first choice had been the ambassador to London, Shigemitsu Mamoru, and the second choice was Tōgō Shigenori, ambassador to Moscow. Abe, however, declared that no one in the Foreign Ministry was suitable and selected Nomura.

After the war, around 1951, the then prime minister Yoshida Shigeru ordered young section heads in the Foreign Ministry to investigate and compile moot points in Japanese diplomacy from the Manchurian Incident, through the second Sino-Japanese War, down to the defeat in the Pacific War, and had the results compiled as reference material for later generations of officials. The document has been preserved and is known today as *Nihon gaikō no kago* (Errors in Japanese diplomacy). One of the questions was about the German-Soviet Nonaggression Pact. The Hiranuma cabinet resigned with the statement about conditions being "complex and mysterious," and all discussion about a tripartite alliance was dropped. Was that enough? *Nihon gaikō no kago* asked. "Looking back on it now, the conclusion of the Pact and the outbreak of war in Europe was Japan's best opportunity to part company with Germany and Italy and return to its own path. There was sufficient reason to do so even from the point of view of international codes of conduct."

Considering when this report was compiled, we cannot ignore the existence of historical hindsight. Nevertheless, it is a fact that in the short period of time between the painful betrayal signified by the German-Soviet Nonaggression Pact and Japan's being misled again the following year by Germany's rapid advances in Europe, there existed a golden opportunity to return Japanese diplomacy to reason.

The gravity of the situation demanded that a foreign minister be chosen who had strong moral fiber and a great amount of experience. Shigemitsu, of all the candidates, would have been the best fit for the position. He had a thorough knowledge of the situation in Europe, having served as ambassador in Moscow and London, and was greatly trusted in British government circles. The elder statesman Saionji Kinmochi said of him approvingly, "Of all the telegrams received recently from ambassadors serving abroad, those of Shigemitsu make the most sense. He's very good." There is, of course, no point in asking "what if?" after the fact, but in view of Japan's subsequent tragic history, I can't help regretting that Shigemitsu's appointment as foreign minister never came to pass.

Japanese-Polish Relations

When we attempt to solve the riddle of Sugihara Chiune, we must not forget the importance of Poland, a large country in Central Europe with a complicated history and a rich culture, as exemplified by Chopin's music. It is not widely known that, from around the time of the Russo-Japanese War through the Second World War, a variety of exchanges took place between Japan and Poland. If we ignore the close relationship between the two, we will not be able to get a clear understanding of the significance of Sugihara's visas or the details of his work as an intelligence officer. I will take the opportunity here to look at the relationship between the two countries, relying on, among others, a study coauthored by Professor Ewa Pałasz-Rutkowska, Chair of Japanese Studies and former head of the Department of Japanese and Korean Studies at Warsaw University, and Lithuanian-born Pole Andrzej T. Romer.[28]

When Japanese speak of the image they have of Poland, they often quote from a Japanese Imperial army song called "Pōrando kaiko" (Remembrance of Poland):[29]

> Reaching the lonely village, I asked, "what is this place?" Poland, they said, sadly destroyed long ago.

The song is based on the memoirs of Major Fukushima Yasumasa (who later became Vice Chief of the General Staff and then a full General), who journeyed back to Japan alone across Poland, Russia, and Siberia in 1892–1893, after serving as military attaché at the Japanese legation in Berlin. It is extremely interesting that Meiji-era Japanese should have had such sympathy for Poland, whose name had been erased from the map, partitioned as it was between Russia, Prussia, and Austria-Hungary.

The seeds of friendship between the two countries were sown at the time

---

28 Ewa Pałasz-Rutkowska and Andrzej T. Romer, *Historia stosunków polsko-japońskich 1904–1945* [History of Polish-Japanese relations 1904–1945] (Warsaw: Bellona, 1996; 2nd enlarged and revised edition, Warsaw: Trio, 2009; 3rd edition, Warsaw: Wydawnictwo Japonica 2019).

29 Lyrics by Ochiai Naobumi, composer unknown.

of the Russo-Japanese War (1904–1905), when the Japanese army took large numbers of Russian prisoners of war. It is well known that the Japanese government, conforming to international law, treated them well. Among them were Polish soldiers drafted into the Russian army. Since there was a risk that they might be treated poorly if imprisoned with the Russians, the government showed its consideration by separating out the Poles and confining them separately.

The reminiscences of Hyōdō Nagao, who served as ambassador to Poland between 1993 and 1997, are also of great interest. He entered the Foreign Ministry soon after the end of the Second World War and was sent to study in Britain. In the aftermath of the war, when there was still a great deal of anti-Japanese sentiment in the country, he says only one teacher showed him great kindness. He thought it strange that this man should be so good to him, and asked why. The teacher replied that he had been born in Poland and that his father, unavoidably conscripted into military service, had been captured by the Japanese and treated very well.

At the time of the Russian Revolution, too, the Japanese had acted in a way that deepened their friendship with Poland. At that time, a large number of Polish political prisoners were exiled in Siberia, where they established communities with their families, who had followed them into exile. The Russian Revolution triggered frequent massacres of Poles, who were regarded as dangerous elements, and as a result, many children were left orphans and faced a desperate future. Worried about the situation, Polish residents of Vladivostok formed a Committee of Rescue in September 1916 and appealed to various countries for help. One of the core members of the committee, Anna Bielkiewicz, went to Japan and, on June 18, 1920, paid a visit to the Foreign Ministry. Hanihara Masanao, the then vice-minister, immediately asked the Japanese Red Cross to help the orphans. Prompt action involving the Foreign Ministry, the Japanese Red Cross, the army and navy, and the Home Ministry resulted in the first group of children leaving Vladivostok just a month later, on July 20, on a Japanese ship bound for the port of Tsuruga in Fukui Prefecture. Altogether, 765 orphans were rescued and returned safely to Poland, despite an epidemic of typhus that broke out among them while they were in Japan. They were treated by Japanese doctors and all of them recovered, but unfortunately a young Japanese nurse taking care of them, Matsuzawa Fumi, lost her life to the disease.

Tsuruga was the same port through which a great many of the refugees who received visas from Sugihara Chiune arrived in Japan some twenty years later. Both events have been commemorated at the Port of Humanity Tsuruga Museum, which is visited today by many people. Since Japan was at the height of its Siberian Intervention in 1920, undertaken to stem the spread of Communism, there was admittedly a political dynamic at work that favored Poland, which had received such cruel treatment from the Soviet Union. But it remains an undeniable fact that Japan's backing of Poland permeates modern history.

Partition of Poland and Resistance

There are also numerous examples illustrating Polish goodwill toward Japan. Particularly striking was the offering of intelligence concerning Europe's international posture after Japan left the League of Nations in 1933 and lost the intelligence gathering opportunities it offered. Poland's diplomatic officials, headed by Foreign Minister Józef Beck, scrupulously notified Japan about what had been discussed at the general assembly of the League and elsewhere, and the circumstances behind those discussions.

In the interwar period, Poland's borders were extremely complicated. Germany lay to the west, its territory divided by the Polish Corridor, a narrow strip of land providing Poland with access to the sea. The Free City of Danzig (now Gdańsk), protected by the League of Nations, lay within it. The German enclave of East Prussia lay to the east, located totally within Poland. Parts of modern-day Belarus and Ukraine were also Polish territory. Large numbers of ethnic Russians lived in Poland, and their presence was later used as a pretext by the Soviet Union for invading. Given its position between Germany and the Soviet Union, Poland made every effort during the interwar period to maintain its independence.

The German-Soviet Nonaggression Pact, regarded by Japan as a betrayal, was of great concern to Poland as well. Poland had more or less maintained a balance between the two great powers until then, but with the conclusion of the Pact, it feared that Germany would make territorial demands of it, unworried by any potential intervention by the Soviet Union. Ambassador Sakō frequently reported Beck's anguish that this would result in war to Kasumigaseki.

An interesting article appeared in the *Tokyo Asahi Shimbun* on August 25 concerning the visit of the Polish ambassador to Japan, Tadeusz Romer, to Sengakuji in Shiba Takanawa, Tokyo, a temple associated with the Forty-Seven Ronin.[30] Today's readers may wonder why such a fuss was made about something so innocuous as a visit to a temple, but perhaps the ambassador wanted to bring Poland's dangerous situation to the attention of the Japanese public by making a pilgrimage to the temple that enshrined the Forty-Seven Ronin, who had bravely faced danger to their own domain. He was likely eager to do whatever he could to arouse the concern of the Japanese.

As the name "Poland" (from *Polska*, a land of flat fields) suggests, the country is flat, with few natural strongholds, making it difficult to defend against invaders. Ambassador Sakō reported that the Poles were a proud people and, if the Germans invaded, they would put up a spirited defense, luring the enemy into regions of lakes and marshes and conducting a protracted war from there in the expectation that the British and French armies would, in time, come to their aid. However, they overlooked two things. The first was the blitzkrieg mobility of the German forces. Hostilities opened on September 1, 1939, with a lightning assault by combined air and land forces. The Polish army, with only old-style aircraft and cannons, suffered defeat everywhere and the German army quickly advanced deep into the interior of the country.

On the other side of Poland was the Soviet Union. Suddenly, as if pre-arranged with Germany, its army struck. The Soviet Union had secured stability in the Far East with the ceasefire with Japan over the Nomonhan Incident on September 15. Two days later, its army attacked Belarus and Ukraine, part of Polish territory. Foreign Commissar Molotov justified the attack as rescuing their "brothers" living in the two territories. As we have seen, there were many ethnic Russians living there, but as was reported in

---

30 The Akō *rōshi*, former retainers (rōnin) of the disgraced lord of Akō domain, vowed to take revenge by killing the man who had brought about this disgrace. Having done so, they committed *seppuku*. Their graves are at Sengakuji. —Trans.

the *Tokyo Asahi Shimbun*, they did not necessarily welcome the Soviet army.

I visited Warsaw for the first time in the summer of 2003 and was shown around by Professor Pałasz-Rutkowska. An eerie monument that she told me had recently been built left a strong impression on my mind. It consisted of a flatcar on rails that bristles with bronze crosses, both Catholic and Orthodox, and other religious symbols. In the center is the date of the Soviet invasion, 17 IX 39, and on the sleepers of the rails are carved the names of places in the East. The monument symbolizes

The Monument to the Fallen and Murdered in the East, Warsaw.

the deportations to the East and resulting deaths of large numbers of Poles after the Soviet invasion and expresses anger that remains strong to this day.

Warsaw fell in the middle of September, and on the 28th, Germany and the Soviet Union signed the German-Soviet Frontier Treaty, partitioning Poland. The Polish government did not surrender, instead forming a government-in-exile, first in Paris and then in London. The people continued to resist in various ways.

Before long, these events would affect Sugihara.

An Ulterior Motive

The Diplomatic Archives of the Ministry of Foreign Affairs contain a document called "Sugihara Chiune's Visa List." It records the names of those who were issued visas while Sugihara was posted in Kaunas and is one of the most noteworthy documents associated with him. It has been loaned for exhibition to various facilities, including the holocaust museums in Washington, Houston, and Illinois.

Visa lists were compiled in response to a May 3, 1937, directive from Foreign Minister Satō Naotake to the heads of diplomatic missions abroad. The directive stated:

"In view of the necessity of managing the entry to Japan of foreign nationals, when missions abroad issue them visas or travel documents, [they should be] numbered in issue-date order and, from April 1 this year, be reported to the Ministry in three-month batches to the end of March, the end of June, the end of September, and the end of December, four times a year in all. The report should be sent by the 10th of the following month. Even if there are no applicants, this should be reported."

This directive was not intended to serve as a means of gathering information about visitors to Japan from Europe, since at the time there was a reciprocal visa waiver system in place between Japan and most European countries: Belgium, Switzerland, France, Italy, Liechtenstein, the Netherlands, Spain, Germany, Sweden, Denmark, Finland, Norway, Austria, Iceland, Estonia, Lithuania, Czechoslovakia, Latvia, and Hungary (in order of implementation). Britain and the Soviet Union were the notable exceptions. This means that, in the first volume of visa application records from Europe (outside of Britain and the Soviet Union), virtually all say "no applicants," and there are some instances when the quarterly reports were submitted after the deadline. As a matter of interest, one report from the Finland legation remains that has the signature "Sugihara Chiune, *chargé d'affaires*." This proves that Sugihara Yukiko was correct when she wrote in *Rokusennin no inochi no biza* that he had served in this post.

In all events, it is no exaggeration to say that, as far as Europe was concerned, there was almost no point in making visa lists when the directive was issued. Why, then, were they necessary? At that time, large numbers of visas and other documents for travel to Japan were being issued to "stateless Russians" (that is, White Russians) at diplomatic offices in China and Manchukuo. The Japanese government's original motivation regarding the lists was to scrutinize trends among them, and particularly to check whether any of the Russians were Soviet spies. The Anti-Comintern Pact had been signed with Germany some six months earlier, and the tightening of Japanese immigration control could very well have been connected to this.

The outbreak of war in Europe changed the situation. The old visa waiver system remained in name only, and many of the Japanese missions in Europe began producing visa lists. The one from Sugihara's time in Kaunas is one such example. Volume 2 (visa lists from Europe) provides us with detailed information about the issuance of visas in wartime Europe. I can still vividly recall Richard Salomon, then vice president of the Illinois Holocaust Museum and Education Center near Chicago, when he visited Japan to borrow materials in conjunction with the opening of the museum. Looking fixedly at Sugihara's list, he said to me, "That's my father's name. That's my uncle. That's my cousin." Speechless for a moment, and with tears running down his cheeks, he then said quietly, "It is because of Sugihara that my family exists." It was a memorable encounter. Mr. Salomon told me he was born after his parents reached the United States, and his birth itself was thanks to Sugihara's visa.

This important document contains 2,140 names. Each entry consists of a serial number, nationality, name, whether the visa was entry or transit (all in the list were transit), date issued, and visa fee (two Lithuanian litas). It is generally said that Sugihara saved six thousand lives. I will touch on why 2,140 people swelled to six thousand below, but for now I would like to concentrate on nationality. Many people perhaps wonder why they cannot find the word "Jewish" on the list, given that Sugihara is said to have saved so many Jews. But "Jewish" refers to ethnicity; Jews lived in many different countries and so had a variety of nationalities. Poland had the greatest number of Jews in Europe at the beginning of the war, said to have numbered between three and four million. When Poland was partitioned between the Soviet Union and Germany, many people fled to Lithuania, including large numbers of Polish Jews. As a result, many of the people saved by Sugihara would have been Jewish.

It is a twist of fate that the issue of Vilnius happened to play such a large role in the escape of Polish refugees. After the First World War, many countries in Europe became independent, and various border conflicts broke out, one of which was between Lithuania and Poland over Vilnius. This city had been built in the Middle Ages by Grand Duke Gediminas, who expanded Lithuanian territory greatly to the east, and it became the capital of the Grand Duchy of Lithuania in 1323. A legend tells how Gediminas, while on a hunting trip on the hill that is now Vilnius, had a dream of a huge wolf clad in iron armor. Taking this as a good omen, he built a city there. This is why souvenirs of an armored wolf are sold there.

We have seen that, after the First World War, a territorial dispute erupted between Poland and Lithuania over Vilnius, leading to the breaking off of diplomatic relations between the two. Today, the population of the city is a multi-ethnic mix, including ethnic Poles, ethnic Russians, and ethnic Ukrainians, to the extent that there is a wry joke that there are fewer Lithuanians living in Vilnius than there are living in Chicago. Today, the city is a model of peaceful multi-ethnic coexistence.

When Poland was partitioned at the beginning of the war, Vilnius was included in the Soviet sphere. The Soviet Union offered to return Vilnius to the Lithuanians, but the Soviets turned out to have a surprising ulterior motive. After the partition, Germany remained quiet for a time, and a period of inactivity called the Phoney War[31] continued on the western front. However, based on a secret protocol in the Nonaggression Pact between the two, the Soviet Union began to reach out to Finland and the Baltic states. After the Polish partition, it entered mutual assistance treaties with the Baltic states, acquiring the right to establish military bases there as the first step toward annexation. This is known as the "first occupation."

The first target was Estonia. It had been left in a weakened position following the escape of the Polish submarine *Orzeł* from Tallinn on September 18, 1939. On September 24, just a week after the invasion of Poland, the Soviet Union called Estonian Foreign Minister Karl Selter to Moscow and criticized him over the submarine incident, questioning Estonia's neutrality, and on the 28th, Selter was forced to agree to a mutual assistance treaty that allowed the Soviet Union to build military bases there.

The next victim was Latvia. Unlike Estonia, there was nothing for which it could be criticized. All the same, on October 2, its foreign minister, Vilhelms Munters, was called to Moscow and forced to agree to a mutual nonaggression treaty that permitted the Soviet Union to establish naval and air bases in the country. Unable to resist, the Latvian government signed it on October 5.

That left Lithuania. The reminiscences of the then foreign minister Juozas Urbšys tell us what happened. He was called to Moscow on October 3, hoping that it might mean the Soviet Union would return Vilnius. His hope

---

31 Also called *drôle de guerre* (strange war) by the French. The Japanese expression *kimyō na heiwa* means "strange peace."

was fulfilled, but at a high price. Since the port of Klaipėda had been seized by Germany, Lithuania had no coastline, so there was no Soviet interest regarding a possible naval base. What the Soviets wanted were permanent military bases in specially designated areas within the country. Urbšys protested, saying that the proposal meant the virtual occupation of Lithuania. Stalin and Molotov smiled faintly and explained that these troops would protect Lithuania's independence if it were attacked. Stalin also said that if a Communist uprising should occur there, the Soviet garrisons would help quell it. Even when Urbšys continued to protest, they showed him little regard, arguing that, whereas Germany had stolen territory from Lithuania, the Soviet Union would return it. Returning home, Urbšys consulted the government. He returned to Moscow with the alternative proposition that Soviet troops would only be allowed into Lithuanian territory if the country were in danger. Stalin and Molotov refused absolutely to listen to Lithuania's proposal, and on October 10, an agreement to return Vilnius to Lithuania and a mutual assistance treaty were signed between the two nations.

Momentarily Opened—a Door to Life

A good example of those whose survival was due to Sugihara Chiune is a Polish Jew called Zorah (or Zerach) Warhaftig, a lawyer from Warsaw who escaped to Lithuania with his pregnant wife and traveled to Japan on a transit visa issued by Sugihara. After the war, he was appointed minister of religions in Israel.

Warhaftig criticized the Soviet return of Vilnius, writing that the Lithuanians "failed to realize how dangerous this Trojan gift would be. The U.S.S.R.'s real purpose was to swallow up 'greater' Lithuania."[32] There is an element of truth in this when we consider the annexation of the Baltic states by the Soviet Union in 1940. Urbšys and the other members of the government nevertheless tried desperately, as we have seen, to circumnavigate the Soviet military presence.

Who benefited the most from the return of Vilnius? It was neither

---

32 Warhaftig, Zorah, *Refugee and Survivor: Rescue Efforts During the Holocaust*, trans. Avner Tomaschoff (Jerusalem: Yad Vashem, 1988), p. 40.

the Lithuanians nor the people of the Soviet Union, but refugees like Warhaftig. When rumors of the return began to circulate, he and others who were fleeing from Warsaw to Lviv in eastern Poland hurried toward Vilnius, thinking that if they arrived there before the handover, they would find themselves in neutral Lithuania before long. The door to freedom they sought was only open for a short time. It was a difficult two-day journey on a packed train from Lviv to Vilnius, but large numbers of Polish refugees succeeded in making their way to Vilnius before the formal handover on October 28, thus escaping to Lithuania.

Sugihara Monument, Holocaust Museum (The Green House), Vilnius.

The relocation of the functions of the capital from Kaunas to Vilnius did not, however, happen overnight. Government offices, foreign diplomatic missions, travel companies, and so on remained, as before, concentrated in Kaunas. Many refugees, including Warhaftig, moved on to Kaunas, where they came across Sugihara. The brief window of opportunity provided by the unfolding territorial issue between Lithuania, Poland, and the Soviet Union allowed large numbers of people to escape before Lithuania closed its borders after the return of Vilnius. I cannot help but think that the word "miraculous" is apposite here.

Like the Film *Casablanca*

Though the Polish people had lost their country, this did not mean that they ceased to resist the occupation. On the contrary, they continued to defy Germany and the Soviet Union with almost unparalleled valor throughout the Second World War. One of the most famous examples is the bravery shown by Polish pilots serving the Polish government-in-exile, who fought in the Royal Air Force during the Battle of Britain and shot down large numbers of German planes.

On the intelligence front, too, Polish army officers were active behind the scenes. Kaunas was at first an important base for them, being situated in a neutral country bordering enemy territory. It was also a center for espionage

Historical Presidential Palace, Kaunas.

where German and Soviet agents operated, themselves the target of intelligence activities. The city was at that time, therefore, a key focal point in the global intelligence war.

The Historical Presidential Palace in Kaunas has several exhibitions, including one related to Antanas Smetona, who was president when Sugihara was posted there. Incidentally, Sugihara's exequatur, the document that granted him permission to exercise office as a consul in Lithuania, was issued in Smetona's name. My attention was once drawn to a map of Kaunas showing the location of the foreign legations and consulates there at that time by their flags. Their number was a vivid reminder of how many diplomats from different countries were working there.

Professor Egidijus Aleksandravičius of Vytautas Magnus University has commented, "This may sound a bit romantic, but Kaunas at that time was a kind of European Casablanca." He is thinking of the film *Casablanca*, starring Humphrey Bogart and Ingrid Bergman, which portrays a complex web of human relationships between people of different nationalities and agendas in the city of Casablanca. Kaunas, too, was swarming with people from many different countries on the intelligence front line.

Lithuania shared borders with Germany and the Soviet Union, and it was not impossible to secretly send intelligence officers across those borders at times. It stood to reason that Kaunas was an important post for Polish intelligence officers. There was a further significant advantage for them. It is said that a wise man hides a leaf in a forest, an ironbound rule for covert actions, and this made Kaunas, flooded with Polish refugees, a good place for Poles to move around without arousing suspicion.

The Japanese tend to overlook the importance of religion. We talk generally of "Christianity," but it is divided into many denominations, including Catholic, Protestant, and Greek Orthodox. We have already seen that Lithuania is the only Baltic country that is Catholic. When we travel south from Estonia and Latvia into Lithuania, we find a very different atmosphere in the towns there. And then going on into Poland (Pope John Paul II was Polish), we find the townscape there reminiscent of Lithuania. The similarity between the two countries sharing a lifestyle based on the Catholic faith must have been an advantage, allowing Polish intelligence agents to blend in.

Sugihara's Intelligence Network

We cannot talk about Sugihara's intelligence network in Kaunas without mentioning the Polish intelligence officers with whom he was in contact. This collaboration between Poland and Japan in intelligence matters at this stage may seem surprising, but we must not forget that the signing of the German-Soviet Nonaggression Pact sharpened Japanese distrust of Germany. Japan had declared its neutrality in the European war, and aided by its good relations with Poland, the foundations had already been laid for cooperation in espionage activities.

Sugihara had built up personal contacts with White Russians from the time he went to Harbin as a Foreign Ministry cadet. In Lithuania, his new sphere of activity, he was also driven by the necessity of establishing new contacts as quickly as possible. In such circumstances, it is not at all surprising that he and the Poles should be drawn to each other and forge a cooperative relationship. This gradually strengthened through contacts with the "Willow Group"[33] and with the Union of Armed Struggle (ZWZ: Związek Walki Zbrojnej), the Polish underground army fighting against both Germany and the Soviet Union. Later the ZWZ even used Japanese diplomatic channels to send reports to the Polish government-in-exile in London.[34]

Even after the partition of Poland, the Japanese government allowed the Polish embassy in Tokyo to continue its operations uninterrupted, on the grounds that Japanese-Polish relations remained unchanged. This was before Japan moved uncompromisingly to Germany's side and explains why Sugihara's intelligence activities were permitted. The reaction of the Japanese government almost suggests it was retaliating against Germany for the Nonaggression Pact with the Soviets that it perceived as a betrayal. But over and above that, it would have assented to Sugihara's activities because it received extremely valuable intelligence in return for the support it provided to Poland, as outlined above. Unfortunately, nothing in the way of telegrams or reports from Sugihara from his time in Kaunas survives, other than materials from 1940 connected with his issuing of visas, due to the fact that a large number of Foreign Ministry records were destroyed during the war.

An exceptional document that has survived is a report concerning conditions in Belarus, a former Polish territory occupied by the Soviet Union. Dated February 27, 1940, it is a communication from Sugihara to Foreign Minister Arita, filed as Official Correspondence (Ordinary) No. 37. It is handwritten, about fifty pages long, and deals with topics such as the history, geography, climate, and industries of Belarus. On first reading, its intelligence value seems low, just a compilation of general statistical information. However, my attention was drawn to the statement in the preamble that the statistics were based largely on data used by Polish government bodies. The fact that Sugihara had acquired this data in Lithuania, a country which

---

33 The "Willow Group" was a Polish intelligence group that had been operating in Lithuania since before the war. Following the 1939 invasion, many Polish troops escaped into Lithuania, where they were interned. The Willow Group played an important role in a network that grew up to organize escapes. Its priority was to extricate former intelligence officers and help them escape to the West. Personal communication from Professor Ewa Pałasz-Rutkowska.

34 Pałasz-Rutkowska and Romer, *Historia stosunków polsko-japońskich 1904–1945.*

for many years had had no diplomatic ties with Poland, combined with the fact that he was able to put together this long report within six months of arriving in Kaunas despite having almost no understanding of the Polish language, strongly suggests that he had Polish cooperation.

Two Polish Agents

Two Polish agents had close ties to Sugihara: Captain Alfons Jakubianiec, a.k.a. Jerzy Kuncewicz ("Kuba"), and Lieutenant Leszek Daszkiewicz, a.k.a. Jan Stanisław Perz. The price for their cooperation was allegedly an official Japanese passport. When Sugihara moved to Prague and then Königsberg, Daszkiewicz continued to work with him.

Another important figure directed the activities of these two agents in the background: Major Michał Rybikowski, a.k.a. Peter [Piotr] Iwanow, a White Russian. He had been decorated for his actions during the Polish-Soviet War of 1919 and 1920, and on the eve of the Second World War, he was a specialist on the Polish General Staff dealing with issues involving Germany. After the war broke out, he traveled to the Baltic states by way of Paris and Helsinki, and made contact with Onouchi Hiroshi, Japanese military attaché in Riga. Onouchi, in agreement with Sugihara, provided him with a passport issued by the Manchurian legation in Berlin. Following the annexation of the Baltic states by the Soviet Union, Onouchi became military attaché at the Helsinki legation and so Rybikowski moved to Stockholm, where he continued to handle Captain Jakubianiec and Lieutenant Daszkiewicz. These men would later play a very important role in relations with Japan that I will cover in the last chapter.

That Sugihara was able to establish such close relations with these men in such a short time is clear indication of his skill as an intelligence officer. However, skilled linguist though he was, he could not speak Polish. How did he communicate with Captain Jakubianiec and Lieutenant Daszkiewicz and all the refugees who later came flooding to the consulate seeking visas? An interesting document exists that perhaps hints at an answer. It is a telegram dated September 11, 1920, after the Japanese legation was set up in Poland, sent by Captain Yamawaki Masataka, who was in Europe on official business. In it, he gave advice on the selection of personnel to the Polish legation, including the minister and legation staff. Concerning language, he said that most Poles understood Russian and German, and it was advisable that staff could communicate in both. He also said that government officials and intellectuals preferred French to Russian and German, but that very few understood English.

Sugihara's linguistic talents were put to good use. Not only did he speak Russian, he had studied German for the Foreign Ministry examination for language cadets and had enough French to draft a rebuttal of the Lytton Report. Sugihara spoke to Captain Jakubianiec and Lieutenant Daszkiewicz in Russian, and considered Jakubianiec's Russian to be superior to that of Daszkiewicz.

It was thanks to his strong linguistic skills and outstanding abilities as an intelligence officer that Sugihara was able to set up an intelligence network in Europe in such a short space of time. This would later prove to be critical to his issuing of visas.

CHAPTER SIX

Solving the Mystery of
the Visas for Life

The Meeting with Solly Ganor

When speaking about Sugihara Chiune during his time in Kaunas, we cannot ignore the testimony of a Jewish boy called Solly Ganor. His book *Light One Candle: A Survivor's Tale from Lithuania to Jerusalem*, published in 1995, is a valuable memoir that has long drawn the attention of researchers. It allows us to catch a glimpse of Sugihara's daily life not found in official documents. An unlikely but beautiful friendship spanning differences in age and nationality grew between Solly, with his love for stamp-collecting, and the diplomat from a faraway country in the east. This friendship makes for a very heartwarming story, but viewed from an intelligence perspective, it takes on a completely different meaning.

The two met at Hanukkah ("festival of lights"), an important Jewish celebration that commemorates the rededication of the Temple in Jerusalem after Jews, led by Judah Maccabee, drove out the occupying Seleucid dynasty of Syria from the city in the second century BCE. The festival has great meaning for all Jews. It falls in December, and Jewish children receive presents from parents and relatives, similar to the Christmas presents exchanged at around the same time. Candles are placed in a special nine-branched candelabrum called the Hanukkah menorah (also called the "hanukkiah") at the beginning of the festival and lit on each of the subsequent eight nights. It is traditional for family and friends to gather together at this time. The seven-branched menorah is used the rest of the year, and it is this that appears in the Israeli coat of arms.

At the end of 1939, there were large numbers of Jewish refugees from Vilnius and all parts of Poland in Kaunas. There is a strong spirit of mutual assistance in Jewish society, and Jewish families living in Kaunas looked after their brethren who had fled there. Solly's family, which had prospered in business, had taken in a father and daughter by the name of Rosenblat who had escaped from Poland. Rosenblat had lived in Warsaw with a wife and two daughters, but their home had been destroyed during an air raid when the Nazis were attacking the city and his wife and elder daughter had been killed. He took his surviving eight-year-old daughter and fled to Lithuania, where Solly's family took them in. Solly's mother and aunt worked in a relief organization for Jewish refugees, and the eleven-year-old Solly, with their example before him, had impulsively donated all ten litas he had received as Hanukkah money to help the refugees. It is not certain how much money this represented, but considering a visa issued by Sugihara cost two litas per person, ten litas would cover the cost for a family of five. Ten litas must have represented a substantial amount of money for the eleven-year-old.

This action, born of a childlike sense of justice, soon led to regret. Solly had forgotten that a Laurel and Hardy film was on. He wanted to go and see it but he had given away all the money he had and his wallet was empty. His father praised him for what he had done, calling it "a splendid act of self-sacrifice," but it was that very sacrifice that made it so special. He refused to give Solly any more pocket money. Solly, who really wanted to see the film, visited his aunt Anushka, who ran a gourmet food store, hoping he could get money from her. A gentleman happened to be there shopping: none other than Sugihara. Solly's aunt introduced them, and hearing about Hanukkah, Sugihara gave the boy some money, telling him to think of him as his uncle. Though a little hesitant, Solly accepted the money and impulsively invited him to come to his family's Hanukkah party, since he was, after all, an uncle. His aunt was taken aback and reprimanded him, saying Mr. Sugihara was a busy man. Sugihara, however, insisted he was not at all busy and happily accepted the invitation.

Considering when this occurred, Sugihara would actually have been extremely busy. He was collecting Soviet intelligence and, in particular, making contact with Polish intelligence agents and sheltering them at times. He also had to send the intelligence he collected off to Japan. Solly's aunt's reprimand to her nephew for issuing this spontaneous invitation was probably also colored to an extent by reluctance to invite a non-believer to such an important religious event.

Sugihara and Yukiko visited Solly's family on the first day of the festival. During the Hanukkah party, Sugihara listened intently to Rosenblat's description of his terrible experiences in Poland and the circumstances of his flight. It is quite clear what this signifies. Solly's invitation must have stirred Sugihara's blood as an intelligence officer and he accepted it eagerly, knowing that visiting the home of a Jewish family would allow him to meet refugees from Poland and enable him to acquire valuable information.

After supplying Sugihara with details about Poland, Rosenblat suddenly implored him to issue him a Japanese transit visa. Sugihara explained that Japanese immigration law required that transit visas could only be issued when the applicant had permission to enter a destination country and also had sufficient funds. He could not issue a visa if those conditions were not met. At this time, the idea of issuing visas to people who could not meet the conditions had apparently not yet occurred to him.

Between Intelligence Officer and Humanitarian

It is noteworthy that, the same evening, Solly's father told Sugihara that he planned to leave Lithuania once he had put his affairs in order and go to the United States, where his brother and sister lived. No one in the family, not even Solly, had known of this. Sugihara urged him to drop everything and do so as soon as possible. In his words that evening, Sugihara showed himself to be an intricate mix of intelligence officer, diplomat, and humanitarian. It was the intelligence officer who acquired information from Rosenblat, and the diplomat who put his country's laws first when refraining from issuing visas to the father and daughter, however deserving they were of sympathy. However, his urging Solly's father to leave Lithuania as soon as possible seems to have sprung from his humanitarian side.

Sugihara had sensed the dangers facing Lithuania, which I will speak more of below. However, as an intelligence officer, he needed to be discreet about warning Solly's father of those dangers. He could not divulge important information that had come to him in the course of his work to a third person, even if indirectly. In his later interaction with Solly, he appears to have struggled to strike a balance between the three sides of his persona. Solly would go on to visit the consulate quite often to collect postage stamps. In the spring of 1940, Sugihara, as he handed over some more stamps, asked Solly to pass on a message to his father. The situation was worsening, he said, and he should leave as soon as possible. Nor had Sugihara forgotten Rosenblat and his daughter. He continued to worry about them, asking Solly whenever they met if Mr. Rosenblat had been able to obtain a visa for some country or other. As Sugihara was the father of two children, the humanitarian within him probably couldn't help feeling concerned for the future of the boy in front of him and for Rosenblat's daughter. According to *Light One Candle*, once Sugihara made up his mind to turn a blind eye to the law, he issued visas both for Solly's family and for Rosenblat and his daughter. The Visa List contains the names of "Mira Rozenblat" (No. 71) and "Stanislaw Rozenblat" (No. 72). *Light One Candle* does not specify their given names, so whether or not they are the same people cannot be confirmed. Hopefully, they survived and found happiness wherever they ended up.

Though Sugihara provided Solly's family with visas, they failed to use them to escape from Lithuania, owing to the invalidation of their Lithuanian passports as a result of the Russian takeover and Solly suddenly falling ill. In June 1941, Germany breached the Nonaggression Pact with the Soviet Union by occupying Lithuania, ousting the Soviet forces stationed there. The family was sent to the Slobodka ghetto in Kaunas and made to work under harsh conditions. Solly's elder brother Hermann was separated from the family before the move into the ghetto. Just before Germany's defeat, Solly and his father were transferred to Dachau, a concentration camp in Bavaria, and then sent to the Tyrol to construct defenses in what is called the Dachau Death March, infamous for the large number of Jews who lost their lives along the way. Luckily, Solly was rescued by soldiers of the Japanese-American 522nd Artillery Battalion. At the time, Solly was barely conscious, and mistook the features of his rescuer for Sugihara, who he thought had come to his aid. Throughout his terrible ordeal, Solly clearly held his memories of Sugihara dear to his heart.

Rescuing Jews from the Nazis?

The interaction between Solly and Sugihara poses another critical question. Sugihara is usually described as "the diplomat who saved 6,000 Jews from the Nazis." The very fundamental question here is whether this statement is really correct.

Here I would like to remind you that, when Solly's father had spoken at the Hanukkah party about going to the United States as soon as his affairs were settled, Sugihara had urged him to forget about putting his affairs in order and get away as soon as possible. Why was Sugihara so adamant about this?

Which countries menaced Lithuania at the end of 1939? Whether or not Nazi Germany was one such country requires investigation. After Germany defeated Poland with its blitz tactics, there was little military action until April the following year, the period of the so-called Phoney War. Thus, at this time, there was no immediate need for Solly's father to abandon the business he had invested so much in and flee Lithuania with his family in order to escape the Nazis.

Germany did not begin its attack on the Soviet Union until June 1941, a year and a half later, but once Lithuania was occupied by Germany, Jews there began to be systematically oppressed, and Solly's family was forced into the ghetto. All the same, it is historical hindsight to say that Sugihara "saved Jews from the Nazis." At the very least, at the time of the Hanukkah festival in December 1939, Lithuania was not under any threat from Germany. Why, then, did Sugihara judge Lithuania to be in danger at that time? To answer this question, we must delve into his mind as an intelligence officer.

During the Phoney War, it was the Soviet Union that was running amok in Europe. According to the secret protocol in the Nonaggression Treaty, following the "first occupation" of the three Baltic countries, Finland—Sugihara's former post—would be targeted. The Soviet Union demanded Finland cede certain strategically important territories, including the Karelian Isthmus. This land was dear to the hearts of the Finns, as exemplified by the Karelia Suite of Jean Sibelius (whom Sugihara met). The Finnish government refused this demand, knowing it could mean war. Sure enough, the Soviet Union invaded Finland on November 30, 1939, in what is called the Winter War.

Finland had two advantages compared with Poland and the Baltic states. First was its topography. Whereas the Baltic countries are relatively flat, Finland has a difficult terrain made up of forests and lakes. Under the command of the Finnish hero Marshal Mannerheim, soldiers manned defensive fortifications. Further, it was winter, with deep snow. Finnish soldiers, knowledgeable about the terrain and wearing skis for swift movement, caused confusion and great damage to Soviet troops who had lost their way in the snow. Fighting bravely, Finland was also aided by international opinion. The League of Nations judged the Soviet Union to have committed a unilateral act of aggression, and expelled it on December 14, the only expulsion of a nation in its history. This was around the time that Sugihara went to the Hanukkah party. Finland had fought courageously, but given the tremendous disadvantages it faced in scale, there was no knowing how long it could sustain its resistance to the Soviets. The League's influence had diminished to such an extent that expelling the Soviet Union was hardly likely to deter it from moving ahead with its plans.

Sugihara, with his thorough knowledge of the Soviet Union, must have realized that the Baltic states would be the next target. He would have known that anti-Semitism was not exclusively a Nazi prejudice; it had been rife in Tsarist Russia and continued in the Soviet Union. He himself had experienced, during his long stay in Harbin, the bad blood between the Jews and the White Russians that often erupted into conflict. His warning to Solly's father was doubtless based on his keen assessment of the situation.

First Stalin, Then Hitler

The fact that Sugihara warned Solly when he visited the consulate in the spring of 1940 that the situation had worsened and his family should leave as soon as possible indicates that Sugihara was already wary of Soviet intentions. Exactly when he gave this counsel is unknown, but considering the fact that Germany's attention was focused on its surge to the west in May 1940, the "worsening situation" probably referred not to the Nazi threat, but to the Soviet Union, which on March 12 that year had forced Finland to surrender, albeit after suffering severe losses. He must have felt uneasy that Soviet eyes were now being turned greedily toward the Baltic countries.

When did Hitler decide to declare war on the Soviet Union? Certainly at the time of the signing of the Tripartite Pact between Germany, Italy, and Japan in September 1940, the Japanese believed that Germany was going to play the role of a faithful broker to form a four-country bloc with the addition of the Soviet Union as a fourth Axis power. The overthrow of the Communist Soviet Union was always in the cards as far as Hitler was concerned, but the trigger for the policy turnaround is considered to have been Molotov's visit to Berlin that November, when proposed spheres of influence were discussed with Hitler and Ribbentrop. The Soviet Union wanted the Bosphorus and the Dardenelles, as well as Bulgaria, a demand that enraged Hitler as excessive, and it was after this that Germany started planning its invasion of Russia, codenamed Operation Barbarossa. It is therefore unlikely that Sugihara was anticipating a German invasion of Lithuania when he warned Solly of troubled times ahead in the spring of 1940.

What concerned Sugihara as an intelligence officer was not the threat of Germany, but that of the Soviet Union under Stalin. It was the Soviet annexation of the Baltic states in June 1940 that persuaded him to consider issuing visas to refugees like the Rosenblats who did not meet the visa requirements, but with whom he sympathized. Thus, in a broad sense, Sugihara could be said to have "saved Jews from the Nazis" during his time in Kaunas, but in a narrow sense, it would more apt to say that he was protecting them from the menace of Stalin.

Lithuania Submits to the Soviet Union

Following the signing of the Mutual Assistance Treaties in September and October 1939, the situation between the Soviet Union and the Baltic states remained comparatively stable. In May 1940, however, the Soviet attitude abruptly hardened. This was due in part to its embarking on the full-scale annexation of the Baltic states following the end of the Finnish war, and also to the incentive provided by the German invasion of the Netherlands and Belgium. The Japanese Foreign Ministry appears to have considered the latter to have been a major influence, but whatever the reason, it was keenly interested in what was happening with both Germany and the Soviet Union.

In reverse order of signing of the Mutual Assistance Treaties, Lithuania was selected by the Soviet Union as its first target. At the end of May, the Soviets complained to Lithuania about the disappearance of some Soviet soldiers stationed there. Foreign Minister Juozas Urbšys states in his memoirs that this was an utter fabrication with no factual basis. Proof of this lay in the fact that the Soviet Union made accusations but did not conduct any investigation. On May 25, Ladas Natkevičius, the Lithuanian ambassador extraordinary and plenipotentiary to Moscow, was called to the Kremlin, where Molotov delivered a diplomatic note saying:

> We are sure that disappearances of Soviet soldiers were brought about by persons under the protection of the Lithuanian authorities.... The Soviet Government proposes to the Lithuanian Government...to take the necessary steps immediately to search for the Soviet soldiers who disappeared and to transfer them to the military authorities of the Soviet bases in Lithuania. The Soviet Government hopes that the Lithuanian Government will take the necessary measures to comply with the Soviet proposals and will not force it to take other measures."[35]

In response to this threat, the Lithuanian government made every effort to settle the incident, but Stalin and Molotov kept up their criticism. Juozas Urbšys was sent to Moscow to try to resolve the situation, and on June 14 was called to the Kremlin by Molotov, who told him he had a very important proposal. This was an ultimatum, threatening that if the Soviet demands were not met without objection or argument by the next morning, military force would be used. These demands were that the people responsible—the minister of the interior and the director of the Security Department—be prosecuted immediately and that the cabinet resign and anti-Soviet policies cease. These two demands alone represented flagrant meddling in Lithuanian domestic politics, but a third demand required that Soviet military units in Lithuanian territory be increased and deployed at important centers around the country. The Soviet Government would wait for a reply until 10 a.m. on June 15.

Urbšys' disquiet was extreme. He had arrived at the Kremlin just before midnight, and by the time the ultimatum had been read, it was already 1 a.m. on the 15th. This left just nine hours for the Lithuanian government to reach a momentous decision that would determine the fate of the

35 Report of the Select Committee to Investigate Communist Aggression and the Forced Incorporation of the Baltic States into the U.S.S.R. Washington: United States Government Printing Office, 1954, p. 319.

country. And furthermore, the Soviets blocked Urbšys and his aides from using the telephone to communicate with Lithuania. They finally managed to get through around dawn, but by then, the only option remaining was unconditional acceptance.

Urbšys, having transmitted his government's answer to Molotov at 9 a.m. on the 15th, conveyed that the Antanas Merkys cabinet had resigned and that General Stasys Raštikis had been appointed to form a new government. The Soviets, however, continued to show no mercy, threatening the Lithuanian government by brazenly accusing it of selecting a new prime minister without consulting them, saying this was proof of Lithuania's continuing hostile policy. The following day, 160,000 Soviet troops advanced into Lithuania.

Valdus Adamkus, who became the Lithuanian president in 1998, describes in his memoirs his impression of the Soviet occupiers through his eyes as a young boy. Everything was shabby—their clothing, their discipline, their armaments. Because of the Soviets' losses during the war in Finland, large numbers of new recruits were necessary to man the forced occupation of the Baltic states, and it may have been impossible to maintain high standards for the soldiers.

President Smetona urged that independence should be protected even if it meant fighting the Soviets, but without the support of the cabinet, he left to seek asylum in Germany. The Lithuanian Communist Justas Paleckis was appointed prime minister on June 17, and on June 21, the Soviet Socialist Republic of Lithuania came into being. A general election was held on July 14–15, but only candidates approved by the Union of the Working People of Lithuania, a Communist party puppet, could stand. On July 21, at the first session of the People's Parliament, Paleckis announced that Lithuania would apply for entry into the Soviet Union. Its petition was officially accepted by the Supreme Soviet at its seventh session on August 3, 1940.

On June 16, the day after Lithuania received the ultimatum from the Soviet Union, Latvia and Estonia were accused of secretly concluding an anti-Soviet military alliance. Events then followed the same course as in Lithuania, with both countries forced to join the Soviet Union. Now all three Baltic states had been annexed.

The Decision to Issue Visas

By June, the Foreign Ministry of Japan was looking cautiously at events in the Baltic states, but was more concerned with how Germany was going to react, and ordered Kurusu Saburō, its ambassador there, to inquire into this. A telegram from him dated June 25 reported that, as far as Germany was concerned, the Soviet moves had nothing to do with them, and Kurusu observed that, however much the Soviet Union oppressed the Baltic states, Germany could only sit back and watch.

In June 1940, the German army had inexorably moved west, taking Paris, and in Japan, moves to ally more closely with Germany took on renewed vigor. Some embraced the faint hope that Germany, fearing a stab in the back as a result of the Soviet occupation of the Baltic states, would consider an alliance with Japan. However, as far as the Germans were concerned, the Soviet annexation of the Baltic states was a course of action predetermined by the German-Soviet Nonaggression Pact and the German-Soviet Frontier Treaty signed the previous year, so it stood to reason that they would watch the Soviet moves without getting involved.

With the full-scale annexation of the Baltic states, the question arose whether the Soviet Union would permit the continued existence of offices such as the Japanese legation to Latvia and Sugihara's consulate in Kaunas. Japan was certainly in favor of having them remain, particularly the legation to Latvia as a consulate-general. When Germany annexed Austria in a comparable situation, the Japanese legation became its consulate-general in Vienna, as did the Prague consulate-general following the partition of Czechoslovakia. However, from the Soviet perspective, Japanese diplomatic offices in the Baltic countries were clearly the front line for anti-Soviet intelligence activities, and there was no reason why they should be permitted to continue. Britain and other countries with diplomatic offices there had acquiesced to their closure, and Japan reluctantly followed suit and agreed to close its legation and consulates by the end of August 1940.

How did Sugihara respond to the annexation of Lithuania by the Soviet Union and the looming closure of the Japanese consulate in Kaunas? According to the unfinished account Sugihara wrote late in life, large numbers of refugees began congregating around the consulate on July 18, a few days after the general election.[36] He said that he communicated with the Foreign Ministry three times, asking whether he could issue visas, but unfortunately these telegrams cannot be found in extant Ministry records. There is a strong likelihood that these were in the file containing records connected with the annexation of the Baltic states, but the file has disappeared. From the later exchange of telegrams, it seems as if, at this stage, the Ministry ordered him to comply with the immigration law; that is, not to issue visas to refugees. This is why, when he later began secretly issuing visas, he adroitly created the illusion of following the Ministry's directive, employing his skills as an intelligence officer against his own Ministry.

Spinning the Web

According to the Kaunas Visa List, Sugihara first began issuing visas in earnest on July 26, nine days from the time refugees started flocking to the consulate. Nevertheless, a telegram (No. 50) he sent on July 28 contains a detailed report focusing on conditions in Lithuania, mentioning that the GPU had attacked the offices of political organizations and that, in addition to important figures in the old government, such as Urbšys and Merkys, many Poles, White Russians, and Jews had also been arrested. It was only at the very end that he casually reported that around one hundred Jews appeared at the consulate every day seeking Japanese transit visas. He made no mention that he was issuing visas, though at this point, he was apparently already doing so every day, fully aware that this would almost certainly become a problem in the future.

In Telegram No. 58, sent on August 7, Sugihara asked the advice of the Ministry about whether or not he could issue visas to people holding passports issued by the former Czechoslovakian government, given that the country had been partitioned in 1939. Its president at the time of the Munich Conference was Edvard Beneš, who had had a long and close relationship with Japan. When Japan found itself in trouble with the League of Nations over Manchuria, Beneš worked, at Japan's request, as an intermediary between the various countries concerned. He had realized at the Munich

---

36 Sugihara, Ketsudan: Gaikōkan no kaisō.

conference that Czechoslovakia had been abandoned by the nations of the world, and went into exile soon after. The bonds that had tied the multi-ethnic state together had been sundered, and as individual ethnic groups clamored ever more insistently for independence, the majority of the country came under German protection and was partitioned in March 1939.

Visa List (Kaunas). (Diplomatic Archives of the Ministry of Foreign Affairs, Japan)

Since there was an issue concerning passports issued by a government that no longer existed in August 1940, when Sugihara sent Telegram No. 58, he was being ultra-careful in asking the Ministry whether or not he could issue visas. Consultation between Japan and Germany resulted in the decision to recognize Czech passports issued by the former government, as long as they were still valid. Sugihara was told he could issue visas to holders of such passports. At the end of this communication, however, he was cautioned that transit visas could not be given to those without an entry permit for a destination country.

Regarding the matter of a destination country, Sugihara was greatly helped by the "Curaçao visa." This was a clever ploy devised by Jan Zwartendijk, the honorary consul of the Dutch government-in-exile in Kaunas, using the fact that the Dutch colonies of Curaçao, an island in the Caribbean, and Surinam (spelling changed to "Suriname" in 1978) in northeastern South America, could be entered without a visa. Inserting this information into a passport provided proof of destination. This was not, in fact, an official entry permit, since the permission of the governor was required to enter, which meant its validity was doubtful. But at the very least, the refugees were given a *pro forma* destination and a lifeline to leave Lithuania. Even though the Netherlands was under German occupation by that time, Zwartendijk's actions were aided by his own determination to rescue the refugees.

But we must remember that, at this stage, the Baltic countries had been annexed by the Soviet Union, not Germany. If Germany, which had already occupied the Netherlands, had been the one to annex them, it would have been difficult for Zwartendijk to have run such a risk.

There is an interesting episode about the Curaçao visa in relation to Zorah Warhaftig. During his time as Israel's minister of religions, he had the opportunity to speak with the Dutch ambassador to Israel, Mr. Kastil. During the Second World War, Kastil had been the governor of Curaçao and Surinam. When Warhaftig asked him if he would have permitted Jewish refugees carrying such permits to land, he immediately replied that he probably would not have done so. This dubious "Curaçao visa" nevertheless provided an effective escape route to fulfill the formal requirement for Sugihara to issue a transit visa.

Between 2,140 and 6,000 People

Sugihara Chiune is called "the diplomat who saved six thousand lives." What is the basis for calculating this figure? A 1969 newspaper report about Sugihara's invitation to Israel says that he saved the lives of around four thousand people. It would be virtually impossible to come up with an accurate figure, given the confused situation of that time, with Lithuania annexed, the consulate closed, and the flood of refugees pouring into Kaunas. As a result, figures other than four thousand have appeared in the media. With the publication of Sugihara Yukiko's book, *Rokusennin no inochi no biza* (Visas for life for six thousand) in 1990, the figure of six thousand became established. More recent investigations by various researchers have put this figure at less than six thousand, but since it will take some time to determine which figure is closest to the truth, I will continue to use the figure of six thousand here.

How did this discrepancy between the 2,140 names on the Visa List and the number of six thousand rescued come about? The standard explanation is that it was possible at the time for all the members of a family to travel on the same visa. It is true that passport and visa-related regulations were somewhat fuzzier then than they are now. If we accept this theory, that a family consisting of two parents and one child could travel on the same visa, we come up with a calculation whereby six thousand lives could have been saved by 2,140 visas.

Where does this theory originate? There is no mention of this in Sugihara Yukiko's *Rokusennin no inochi no biza*. The basis for the disseminated figure is also unclear in related publications. Was it in fact possible for all family members to travel on the same visa? In my investigation into this fundamental and important question, I have found compelling proof to support this proposition.

At present, there is only one original example of Sugihara's "visa for life" in Japan. As I mention in the Prologue, these visas were very important to those whose lives they saved, and most people have carefully preserved them and are unwilling to relinquish them. However, there is one woman who donated her passport with its visa to the Chiune Sugihara Memorial Hall in Yaotsu (a town in Gifu Prefecture with deep-rooted connections to the Sugihara family), in the hope that it will enable more Japanese to learn about Sugihara. That woman is Dr. Sylvia Smoller, who now lives in New York.

Dr. Smoller was six and living with her parents in Warsaw when the city was attacked by the German army. Escaping to Lithuania, they acquired a Sugihara visa, traveled to Vladivostok on the Trans-Siberian Railway, and crossed by sea to Tsuruga, Japan. Dr. Smoller says she still remembers the kindness they received from the Japanese people during their several months' stay in Japan.

The passport contains the names of her father, mother, and herself, with photos of each. The visa list, however, contains just one name: her father, Aleksander Hafftka (No. 459, issued July 31). Here, then, is an example of one visa being issued to a family. Nevertheless, visas could also be issued individually, as in the case of Zorah Warhaftig: visa No. 454 was issued to his wife, Naomi, and visa No. 455 to himself. There are also many examples in the Visa List of a series of names with the same surname, suggesting members of the same family. Which of the two should be considered standard?

Dr. Sylvia Smoller's visa. (Chiune Sugihara Memorial Hall)

Let us look at the example of the late Edith Hamer, a survivor whom I met, who was born in Kaunas. Her family received a visa from Sugihara in Kaunas and traveled to the United States by way of Japan. I met her when she was acting as a docent at the Holocaust Museum in Houston, telling her own story to visitors so it might be passed down to later generations. When she visited Japan in 2005, she brought her mother's passport, unmistakably stamped with Sugihara's visa. I will never forget how moved I was to actually touch one of his visas for the first time.

There was a swastika on the cover of the passport, and on the first page was stamped a bright red "J". This letter is a feature of all passports issued by Nazi Germany to Jews, but it was a jolt to see the real thing in all its rawness. On the same page was the name of Edith's mother, Sophie Finkelstein, and after it a note saying she was accompanied by one child. Sophie's photograph was on the second page, and on the third, under the heading "Kinder" (children), the name "Edith (Edita)" was entered. The Visa List for July 24 includes Louis Finkelstein (No. 7) and Sophie Finkelstein (No. 8). Edith confirmed that Louis was her father's name. So here we have a case of two visas being issued for three people.

Rokusennin no inochi no biza also notes that accompanying children must have increased the number of those saved, over and above the visa list entries. As in the Finkelstein case, it seems that it was fairly standard to include children in a parent's passport. In other words, it was not a given that one family could travel on one visa; rather, if a child or children were included in the passport, a visa would cover all named in that passport.

Sending the Visa List

Assuming there were six thousand people saved, there would have needed to be an average of around two children per 2,140 passports, but this immediately poses problems, as it is difficult to think that everyone was married with children.

Looking at the Kaunas Visa List without any prior knowledge, you cannot help noticing one oddity. Comparing the daily number of visas issued, very few were issued after August 22. What does this indicate?

When I asked Mrs. Sugihara directly about this, she replied that by the end of August, when the consulate was about to close, the number of visa applicants had, if anything, been increasing rather than decreasing. In *Rokusennin no inochi no biza*, she writes that at the beginning of August, Sugihara had stopped giving numbers to the visas he issued and so the exact number of visas is unknown. Yet the Visa List records Nos. 1 to 2,140. Is there any logical way of explaining this conundrum?

Here we need to look at both Mrs. Sugihara's role and the process by which the Visa List was compiled. First, Sugihara did not involve his wife in the work of issuing visa out of fear for her future safety, so we need to bear in mind that she did not witness the issuing of visas up close. Second, as we shall see, the Visa List was not put together in Kaunas but in Prague, Sugihara's next posting, and the process by which it was compiled very likely holds the key to unlocking the numbers riddle.

After the Kaunas consulate closed, Sugihara departed for Berlin, where the Japanese embassy was located, and was appointed acting consul-general in Prague. While he was in Prague, the large number of people entering Japan on his visas started to become a problem. Many of the refugees were staying in Japan either with no permission to enter a destination country or with insufficient funds to travel onward. Concerned, the Foreign Ministry sent a telegram (No. 10, dated February 4, 1941) to Sugihara in Prague, requiring information about the total number of visas he had issued in Kaunas, and particularly the number he had issued to Jewish refugees. He immediately replied by telegram (No. 12, dated February 5) reporting a figure of 2,132 visas, about 1,500 of which were issued to Jewish travelers. On February 28, he sent the list of those persons issued visas in Kaunas, containing 2,140 names, attached to his regular official correspondence (No. 28). It had taken almost a month to send it, and it now contained eight more names than in the telegram. What was Sugihara doing during this time?

The answer is revealed in the official letter Sugihara sent on February 28. There he explains that the delay in providing the information the Ministry required was due to the pressure of the work involved in closing down the Prague consulate-general and making preparations for the new consulate-general in Königsberg. This is a convincing explanation: Sugihara moved to Königsberg and opened the consulate-general there in March, and this, combined with closing down the Prague office, prevented him from clearing up the remaining business from his former post in Kaunas and sending the required list. The bigger issue here is, did he then possess enough data to enable him to compile the list? The official letter states that the "visa report" would follow by separate post. What does this refer to?

The list of visas issued during his posting in Prague was sent to the Ministry after his move to Königsberg. His official correspondence (No. 17) at that time also mentioned that the visa report would be sent by separate mail. This letter and the attached reports were filed together. The visa report from Prague lists the applicants one by one, with their name, nationality, passport number and date of issue, occupation, family, and reason for journey. There were even photographs attached. It was because Sugihara had brought documentation to Prague that he had been able to compile the list. Since, however, the Kaunas consulate had been closed amid extreme confusion, eight names could have been left off due to lack of time to process the records. This discrepancy perhaps points to the chaos surrounding the last days in Kaunas.

I will discuss the problem of visas issued in Prague in detail below, as it deserves special mention.

The Broader Picture

When we sort through the information we have been able to verify so far, we get suggestions of a broader picture. Just as he would later do in Prague, Sugihara initially recorded detailed information on the issuance of visas in Kaunas. However, at the beginning of August 1940, due to the sheer number of refugees, his records became greatly simplified. Mrs. Sugihara's recollection that visa numbers were no longer attached perhaps means that Sugihara ceased taking precise records. He probably continued issuing visas and switched to jotting down simple notes, but even then was unable to keep up. On August 16, he received a telegram (No. 22) from the Ministry ordering him to strictly observe the Immigration Law. It was probably because he did not even take notes after August 22 that the daily total contained in the list decreased so markedly after this date.

Why, then, did he not completely stop taking notes? Why did a few visas continue to be recorded on the list each day? I mentioned before that Sugihara had strived to create an illusion to mislead the Ministry, and we can catch a glimpse of its traces in the Kaunas Visa List. For example, thinking it strange that no visas were issued on one day in seven (July 21 and 28; August 4, 11, and 18), I discovered that these were Sundays, which implies that the consulate was not open. When I asked Mrs. Sugihara about this, she told me that large numbers of people crowded to the consulate even on Sundays and visas continued to be issued.

It is common practice in historical research not to accept at face value the testimony of those concerned and their families, but in this case, it seems to be as Mrs. Sugihara remembered, based on the fact that most of those people who beat a path to the consulate were Jewish. Their Sabbath (Shabbat) begins on Friday evening and continues into Saturday, and during this time all work activities are forbidden, to the extent they cannot even put up an umbrella if it is raining. Since they gathered around the consulate seeking visas even on the Sabbath, it is not difficult to imagine that they would have been there on Sundays, too.

All the same, the danger remained that a visa dated Sunday might give rise to suspicion that it was false, since the consulate should have been closed for business on that day. As such, Sugihara may have compiled the list to make it appear as if no visas were issued on Sundays. Similarly, if we tentatively assume that the list was terminated on August 21, any visas issued after that date might not be recognized, so Sugihara may have noted down a few names each day and added them to the list to complete the illusion. This supposition is based only on circumstantial evidence, but I think it is reasonable.

One large question still remains: Where did the "visa report" which was to be "sent by separate post" end up? Unfortunately, I have absolutely no idea about this. If it arrived at the Ministry, it should have been filed in the same way as reports sent from the Prague consulate-general, but if it was too big, it may have been filed separately and so is perhaps still sleeping somewhere among Ministry records. It is also very possible it may have met some accident en route in the uncertain conditions of the Second World War and never arrived. Another possibility is that Sugihara himself vacillated over sending it because he had made various adjustments to it. All we can say at this stage is that we may never know the answer.

Leo Melamed's Visa

The telegram (No. 22) sent from the Ministry on August 16, while Sugihara was still issuing visas, and Sugihara's reaction to it are important for the light they cast on the essential nature of his visas.

The telegram said that, among Lithuanians in possession of Japanese transit visas issued by the Kaunas consulate to the United States and Canada, there were those who had not completed entry procedures for their country of destination or did not have sufficient funds for their onward journey. The Ministry wrote that the arrival of such refugees put it on the spot, since they could not be given permission to land in Japan, and ordered Sugihara to strictly observe the regulations for issuing visas from then on.

By this date, then, a steady stream of people issued with Sugihara's visas were already arriving in Japan. Since it took around two weeks to travel

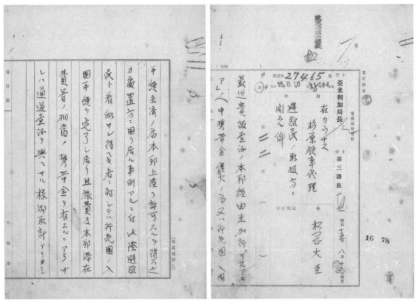

Telegram No. 22. (Diplomatic Archives of the Ministry of Foreign Affairs, Japan)

between eastern Europe and Japan at that time, it makes perfect sense that those who had received visas in the latter part of July would have been turning up on Japanese shores by then. The Ministry's reaction was probably not unexpected as far as Sugihara was concerned, and there is evidence to support this supposition.

Leo Melamed is a Polish-born Jew. He escaped to Lithuania with his parents and went to the United States via Japan on a Sugihara visa. After the war, he became a leading figure in American financial circles, serving as chairman of the Chicago Mercantile Exchange. Professor Teshima Ryūichi was inspired by an interview with Melamed to write the novel *Sugihara darā* (Sugihara dollar), whose main character was based on him. Leo Melamed is famous as the pioneer of financial futures. Amid the chaos of Black Monday in October 1987, when stock exchanges all over the United States ceased trading, only the Chicago Mercantile Exchange continued to trade as normal. When Professor Teshima asked him the reason, Melamed replied, "Whatever the financial tsunami, I never considered closing the market. That's because I'm a Sugihara survivor." Teshima commented on this, saying:

> Having survived the clutches of the two most brutal totalitarianisms of modern times, Stalinism and Nazism, through the Sugihara visa for life, free trade is for him the highest form of surety for the market. It is this very freedom that is at the root of what makes America America. He was an early pioneer of futures trading, and could not conceive of closing down with his own hands Chicago Mercantile, the vanguard of freedom, the cutting edge of capitalism.

It was exactly because Melamed had experienced the oppression of Hitler and Stalin that he was so passionate about the nobility of freedom. To have continued normal trading on the exchange in a way that might have been thought reckless in the midst of a financial crisis was perhaps an embodiment of his fight to preserve freedom. What conveys this most clearly is the expression "Sugihara survivor." Incidentally, when Leo Melamed visited Japan in 2014, he paid a courtesy call to the prime minister, Abe

Shinzō, and told him that everything he had achieved would have been impossible without the actions of Sugihara, words that apparently gave the prime minister a fresh appreciation of Sugihara's great influence. Melamed also had an emotional meeting with members of Sugihara's family and visited the port of Tsuruga, where he had first landed in Japan, and Waseda University, which Sugihara had attended.

When I checked the visa that Melamed continues to prize (his name was included in his mother's passport), a number of important points became apparent. When Sugihara first began issuing visas, he wrote them all out

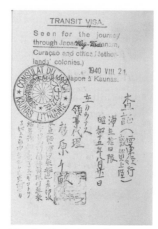

Visa for Mr. Melamed. (Courtesy of Leo Melamed)

by hand, but by the time the Melamed family received theirs, most were stamped, with the exception of such details as the date and destination. Even Sugihara's signature was a stamp. This seems significant because it would have allowed a large number of visas to be issued in a short span of time.

Since Sugihara would not have had the time to get this stamp made himself, the question of who did is of great interest. According to an investigation by Professor Pałasz-Rutkowska, it was made by Poles who traced Sugihara's signature. So here again we have evidence of Japanese-Polish collaboration.

It is difficult to put all the information needed for a visa into one stamp. Looking at Melamed's visa, we find, outside the official consulate seal, that a minimum of four different stamps have been made. One in particular is extremely important. It says: "This visa is issued based on the undertaking that an entry permit for the destination country will be obtained before the ship to Japan is boarded at Vladivostok and that bookings for the ship leaving Japan have been completed." This wording gave Sugihara a pretext to continue to issue visas after he had been ordered in Telegram No. 22 to strictly observe the visa issue regulations. He did not, in fact, reply to this telegram before the consulate closed, and continued issuing visas even to refugees who could not meet the requirements. This text was a special measure that served as the justification for issuing a visa in exchange for an undertaking to arrange an entry permit later.

Sugihara's Second Decision: The Miraculous Illusion

On the other hand, there is a strange thing about the Melamed family's visa. The parents' names appear on the Visa List on August 12, even though the visa was actually issued on August 21. At the moment, there is absolutely no clue why this should have been so, and so we need to collect more information from surviving visas.

Whichever date is correct, however, it provides evidence that Sugihara had already foreseen that he would receive a telegram in the nature of Telegram No. 22. If the Melamed visa had been issued on August 12 as the List states, it means the stamp containing the special measure text had already been made, and even if the visa was issued on August 21 as it appears in the passport, it is difficult to think that the stamp could have been prepared, however hurriedly, in just a few days. This suggests that Sugihara expected such a telegram to be sent and had the stamp made in preparation for such a contingency.

In any case, deciding to continue to issue visas after receiving this telegram would have required tremendous resolve on Sugihara's part. His initial decision to do so in the latter part of July had not been made lightly, considering it meant risking his job. But to continue to do so after receiving Telegram No. 22 was even more perilous, and he took the plunge in full knowledge of the far greater danger, that his action would be branded as a blatant violation of the directive he had received.

However, even if Sugihara continued issuing visas knowing this, his action would have been no more than self-satisfaction if they had not been recognized as valid. His sharpened instincts as an intelligence officer probably perceived the danger that if he completely ignored Telegram No. 22, any visas issued after August 16 would be treated as invalid. If this happened, it would be the refugees arriving in Japan with the visas who would suffer the most. As such, it was crucial that he should appear, to the greatest extent possible, not to be blatantly disregarding the directive, and the special measure stamp was the idea he came up with to serve this purpose.

In appearing not to be disobeying the Ministry's directive, he was motivated not so much by the need to protect himself but rather to safeguard the refugees who depended on him. The special measure stamp was indispensable in creating the illusion that he was observing the Ministry's regulations, an illusion that enabled him to work a miracle.

The Puzzling Telegram No. 66

Sugihara delayed replying to Telegram No. 22 and continued issuing visas, but he did not neglect to probe the Ministry's stance. On August 24, he sent the very mysterious Telegram No. 66, asking whether he should issue a visa to a man named Leon Polak. This puzzling communication excites curiosity, since it seems to have an intent that differs from the tenor of the text.

Leon Polak, a fifty-four-year-old Polish Jewish manufacturer, had escaped to Lithuania with his wife and children, intending to traveling to the United States together. In February of that year, his cousin in New York had submitted an application to the American government for an entry permit for them. His wife and children, who had started the process about a month earlier than him, had received their visas on August 1 from the United States legation in Kaunas and had already received their Japanese transit visas. Polak expected to be issued the same visa, but the United States legation had closed down on August 17 and his prospects were looking bleaker with every passing day. He wanted to leave with his wife and children and wait in Japan for the visa to enter the United States, and asked to be given a transit visa for Japan as a special favor. He had sufficient travel funds and there did not seem to be any suspicion about his explanation. Sugihara, therefore, asked if it would be permissible to issue a visa.

At first reading, this seems to be simply an administrative issue. However, Sugihara had already been issuing a large number of visas that did not comply with the Ministry's regulations, and was in receipt of Telegram No. 22 by this time. The first puzzle here is why he sent this insouciant telegram.

A Trial Balloon

There is a further mystery. According to the Visa List, a man called Leon Polak was issued a visa on August 2 (No. 836). It is not impossible that this man and the Leon Polak of Telegram No. 66 were different people. However, I would like to offer a hypothesis based on the assumption that they were one and the same.

Sugihara was continuing to issue visas on his own initiative to people who did not fulfill the requirements of the Japanese immigration law, despite the fact he had been forbidden to give visas to those who posed a risk of remaining in Japan. What crossed his mind when he saw the telegram of August 16? He could, of course, have abandoned the refugees flocking to the consulate and just left Lithuania, but he did not. The sharp instincts of an intelligence officer made him realize the danger that all the visas he had issued would be declared invalid if he completely ignored the Ministry's directives.

After Telegram No. 22 arrived, he knew that he had to come up with some kind of gambit to ensure that the visas he issued would be valid, and what finally came to mind was Polak's case. When the visa had first been issued, Polak had not received the entry visa for the United States but expected to receive it in the next few days, and he also had sufficient funds for his journey. Compared with many other refugees, he met the conditions for a transit visa. By bringing up his case in Telegram No. 66, Sugihara was perhaps trying see if there was room for the Ministry to make a wider interpretation of the immigration law. This telegram may be considered a kind of trial balloon to gauge the Ministry's reaction. Incidentally, there may have been a connection between this telegram, sent on August 24, and the sudden decrease in the number of visas on the list after August 22.

The Ministry replied to Telegram No. 66 with Telegram No. 23 on August 28, telling Sugihara to issue a transit visa for Polak only after he had received his entry visa for the United States. Though Sugihara had informed the Ministry the American legation in Kaunas had already been closed, the Ministry remained inflexible. He did not reply to Telegram No. 22 until after he closed down the consulate, and in the meantime, he doggedly continued to issue visas to refugees. According to Mrs. Sugihara, the consulate was closed on August 28. Though the last date on the Visa List is August 26, the frantic issuing of visas must have ended on August 28 at the latest.

Putting the Final Touches to the Illusion: Telegram No. 67

Though the consulate was closed and no more visas were being issued, Sugihara still had an important task remaining—his reply to Telegram No. 22. He had to put the final touches on the illusion he had created to ensure the large volume of visas he had issued would be considered valid. This was Telegram No. 67, sent on September 1. Bearing its importance in mind, I will quote its main section in full:

> Re Your Telegram No. 22.
>
> Some refugees in this country have applied for a visa to Japan, now the only transit country available, because there are no Central or South American representative offices nearby and because they expect our consulate to be closed soon. A Japanese visa is also an absolute requirement of the Soviet Union when refugees apply to leave for the United States. In consideration of the circumstances, I have issued visas only to those introduced to me by a reliable person and who undertake to obtain an entry permit to the country of final destination, and have booked a ticket for their onward journey beyond Japan by the time they leave Vladivostok for Japan. As regards funds, they will inform the Tsuruga immigration office in advance, because of exchange control, when they arrange to have money remitted to Japan from abroad. Please be aware that, in response to the need, I am issuing visas based on the above conditions…

The most important part of this telegram is the latter half, from "I have issued visas…" to "… money remitted to Japan from abroad." Although a new condition—arrangements for travel funds—has been added, it is otherwise basically the same as the contents of the special measure stamp that is found on the visa of Leo Melamed. Here Sugihara is reporting that he was issuing visas based on compliance with the special conditions outlined.

Let us consider why Sugihara sent this telegram. The extant text is dated August 1, but this date is unlikely considering it was a reply to a telegram sent on August 16. The date was very probably a transcription error for September 1 that was made when it was copied out at the Ministry. The date is significant.

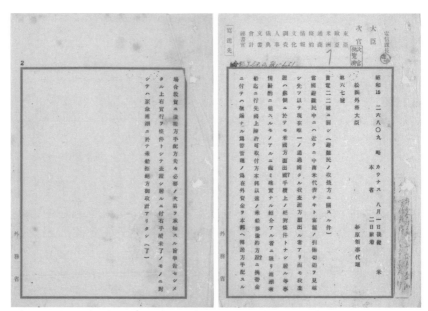

Telegram No. 67. (Diplomatic Archives of the Ministry of Foreign Affairs, Japan)

As we have seen, this telegram was sent after Sugihara ceased issuing visas, but there is another important point about it. It took about two weeks to travel between Lithuania and Japan. The telegram, therefore, needed to reach the Ministry before refugees with visas issued after August 16 began arriving in Japan, otherwise the special measure stamp could lose its meaning. The telegram of September 1 was cutting it very fine. Before then, even if refugees had visas with this stamp, it stands to reason that it would not have made much sense to the Japanese authorities. Explaining the special circumstances surrounding the Soviet annexation of Lithuania, particularly the consequent closure of foreign consulates, and that a Japanese transit visa was the one lifeline for the refugees, Sugihara concluded that they deserved sympathy and included a text similar in content to that of the special measure stamp.

Here, Sugihara was by no means ignoring Telegram No. 22, but based on its content, was rather soliciting the Ministry's understanding for his reasons for issuing visas with attached conditions on the grounds that their circumstances deserved special consideration. It was only with the receipt of this telegram that the Ministry would become aware of the significance of the special measure stamp. A further point to note is that, even though he had already stopped issuing visas, he used the present continuous tense in the telegram as if he were still doing so. Ordinarily in a report about past events like this, we would expect the past tense used, and also some kind of wording seeking approval for having taken a special measure. Sugihara's use of the present continuous tense here is one more example of the finesse with which he dealt with such matters.

Sugihara's greatest fear was that the special circumstances his telegram made a case for would be roundly rejected. He had to avoid getting a negative response to his arbitrary visa issue. By using the present continuous tense, he seems to be aiming at creating a sense of urgency, making the Ministry think that it needed first and foremost to stop the further issuing of visas.

When the Ministry received the telegram on the morning of September 2, it drafted a reply the same day and sent it the next as Telegram No. 24. It said that there were problems in dealing with the refugees described in his telegram and he was warned to "henceforth" strictly observe the regulations laid down in Telegram No 22. Sugihara must have shouted for joy on receiving this. He had elicited the word "henceforth," which, even if it carried the connotation that no more such visas would be tolerated, also implied that the Ministry had little choice but to accept the visas already issued.

The telegram made no mention of what was to be done with Sugihara. He was already prepared for some kind of punishment, but at the very least, the telegram recognized the validity of the visas he had issued. By not totally defying Telegram No. 22 but taking the position that the visas had been issued based on a broad interpretation of it, Sugihara was able to get the Ministry to recognize, albeit reluctantly, that his visas were valid. With his Telegram No. 67, Sugihara had applied the final touches to an illusion that embodied his shrewdness.

The Final Stratagem

The consulate was closed down on Soviet orders. The official stamp, essential for issuing visas, was sent to Berlin, making any further issuance impossible. However, large numbers of refugees remained in Kaunas without any visa. It was then that Sugihara embarked on an action unthinkable to the average diplomat. He went and spent several days at the Hotel Metropolis, saying he needed to rest, and there began issuing travel permits in lieu of visas. He left a notice on the door of the consulate building saying where he was staying, and refugees started to flock to the hotel.

The Hotel Metropolis, Kaunas.

The Metropolis is a long-established hotel that still stands in the center of Kaunas. When I visited Kaunas for the first time in 2002, I contacted the director of Sugihara House beforehand and asked him to find out whether the hotel still had the guest registers from that period. On behalf of the hotel, he replied that unfortunately, due to frequent changes of ownership, registers from the time of the Second World War could not be found. The Visa List ended on August 26, as we have seen. However, it is, as has been verified, incomplete, and I wanted to get independent proof of the date the visas were last issued and the date when the consulate was closed. To know the days on which Sugihara stayed at the Metropolis would, I thought, provide me with a valuable hint, but regrettably nothing could be confirmed. Incidentally, when I visited Kaunas again in 2010, I called the hotel. The staff were delighted to know that their hotel had such an important history. Perhaps before long it will be visited by people from all over the world who have an interest in Sugihara.

Mrs. Sugihara mentions that the consulate was closed on August 28. Since they left Kaunas on either September 4 or 5, the hotel stay seems to have been a little prolonged. A telegram from Sugihara reports that he closed the consulate on September 4 and that he departed for Berlin that same evening. It makes no mention at all of any hotel stay, and the evening departure also makes no sense, suggesting that here, too, Sugihara may have been creating an illusion.

An evening departure was unlikely in view of the fact that he continued to issue travel permits after he left the hotel, in the waiting room of Kaunas Station and from the window of the train before it left. This was attested to not only by Mrs. Sugihara, but also in an interview by the *Chunichi Shimbun* of the brother of Jadvyga Ulvydaite, the tenant who lived on the top floor of the building leased by the consulate. He had seen Sugihara at the station, surrounded by refugees and writing out travel permits, but could not call out to him because of the crowd. Both testimonies speak of a daytime rather than a nighttime departure. At the time, Sugihara's eldest son, Hiroki, was three; his second son, Chiaki, was two; and his then youngest son, Haruki, had just been born (on May 29, 1940). A daytime departure would have been normal in those circumstances.

This is only based on conjecture, but the Ministry's Telegram No. 24 in reply to Sugihara's Telegram No. 67 was sent on September 3, and it should have reached Sugihara the same day, since Lithuania was several hours behind Japan. That he had been able to prolong the broader application of the immigration law to this point seems to have been an outcome that he had planned. The telegram had arrived after the consulate was closed, and there was a strong possibility that the visas he had issued would be recognized as valid, pending discussion over the extension of the immigration law.

The permits Sugihara issued so feverishly while at the hotel had the result of making travel possible, but that was the only result. Mrs. Sugihara remembers that permission to travel based on the permits must have been given "amid the confusion" of war. There was a danger that issuing large numbers of documents, not knowing if they would be valid or not, might have created further problems over and above those related to the issuance of visas, and he may have reported in the telegram that he had left on the evening of September 4 to minimize, even a little, the period he had been writing travel permits.

Seeking the True National Interest

In any event, why did Sugihara go ahead and give out these risky travel permits, even passing them from the train window, when the issuing of visas alone was already fraught with danger? In Telegram No. 67, Sugihara wrote that the Soviet authorities required a Japanese travel visa as an absolute condition for processing applications to leave the country for the United States and claimed that the refugees' situation merited sympathy.

Again, I would like to stress that Lithuania was then under Soviet control, not German. We have seen already in Telegram No. 50, sent by Sugihara on July 28, that Jews were being arrested at the same time as Poles, White Russians, and members of the former government. It appears to have been difficult to convince the Ministry of the extreme dangers faced by Poles and Jews in Lithuania at the time. The difference in the degree of interest between those in the field and at the Ministry was a very difficult problem to solve at that time.

Today, events of this magnitude are reported from the ground by live television and other media platforms, letting the world know what is happening almost in real time. In 1940, the Sugiharas were the only Japanese living in Lithuania, and it was extremely difficult to convey the seriousness of the situation by telegram alone. The fact that the large numbers of Polish Jews who had fled there were in extreme danger from the Soviet Union, where anti-Semitism was rife, was beyond the Ministry's comprehension.

What was behind Sugihara's continued issuance of visas and travel permits, hampered as he was by this information gap? A salient hint can be found in the unfinished account that he wrote in his later years. "Would it have been wise to deny visas and incur the eternal resentment of the Jewish people, with their tremendous hidden influence throughout the world, on the grounds that their documentation was incomplete or that they might pose a risk to public order? Was it really in the national interest to do so?"[37]

What is a diplomat in the first place? Sugihara deliberately used the word in the title of his memoir. A diplomat is a person standing at the front line of relations with foreign countries, representing his or her own country and contributing to its national interest.

Most of those who received Sugihara visas traveled on the Trans-Siberian Railway to Vladivostok and then by ship across the Sea of Japan to Tsuruga in Fukui Prefecture. Interested to know what kind of people they were, I

---

37 Sugihara, Ketsudan: Gaikōkan no kaisō.

asked Inoue Osamu, a local historian, about what had happened at the time. He told me that earlier arrivals looked comparatively neat and tidy, but as time passed, they landed in an increasingly sorry state, with no luggage and no soles on their shoes. At that time, Tsuruga was known as the "Gateway to Europe," with many foreign people passing through, and local residents were consequently used to seeing them, but those arriving on Sugihara visas had the air of vagrants and even seemed a little frightening.

Sugihara firmly believed that giving these people a helping hand would prove beneficial to Japan in the future, and his actions indeed demonstrated outstanding foresight grounded in the keen grasp of international affairs that he had honed during his years as an intelligence officer.

CHAPTER SEVEN

Prague

The Rumor of a Recall to Japan

Leaving Kaunas, Sugihara was ordered to Berlin. He went to the Japanese embassy there, apprehensive that his issuance of visas might be regarded as problematic. However, contrary to his fears, Ambassador Kurusu Saburō made no mention of it. According to Yukiko's memories, Kurusu simply ordered Sugihara to Prague as acting consul-general. Yukiko's recollection that Kurusu did not reprimand her husband must be true in view of the fact that Kurusu himself was an extremely competent intelligence officer who had great hopes for Sugihara.

Unfortunately, Kurusu has been mistakenly regarded as being pro-Nazi. This view has its origins in that he was one of the signatories, as the Japanese ambassador in Berlin, of the Tripartite Pact between Germany, Italy, and Japan, concluded on September 27, 1940, after Germany had dazzled the Japanese government with its swift advance into western Europe. Nevertheless, as we have seen in Chapter 4, Kurusu, acting in concert with his good friend Yoshida Shigeru, ambassador to Great Britain, sent numerous telegrams to the Ministry warning of the danger of an alliance with Germany. It is therefore unreasonable to call him pro-Nazi.

Many surviving documents attest to Kurusu's accomplishments as ambassador to Belgium (June 1936–December 1939). According to him, those in government circles in Belgium, as well as various countries' diplomats based there, regarded Japan as having little interest in European issues. This made it fairly easy to acquire important intelligence, and he was accordingly able to pass on a variety of information about the situation in Europe to the Japanese government. Though this view of Japan by Western diplomatic sources worked in Kurusu's favor, it was a sign of his own ability that he could extract what was important from it. His own excellent feel for intelligence would have told him that Sugihara would be ideal in Prague as an antenna for picking up intelligence on the Soviet Union. Kurusu's overlooking Sugihara's issuance of visas in Kaunas should perhaps be regarded as a result of Sugihara's clever alibi and Kurusu's belief in Sugihara's talents.

At that time, an interesting statement suggesting the risk of punishment Sugihara faced was made by a man central to Japan's plan regarding the Jews, Colonel Yasue Norihiro. He was one of the Japanese army's Jewish experts, and at the time Sugihara was in Kaunas, Yasue was director of the Special Service Group in Dairen (Dalian today). He worked on a grand plan to open up sites in Manchuria for Jews fleeing Europe; in other words, to create a "Jewish state." Once, he was visited by a trading company employee called Furusaki Hiroshi, who recorded this episode in an autobiography written after the war.[38] Furusaki was then working for Mitsui Bussan (Mitsui and Co.) and had been sent to Manchuria in connection with the development of a mercury mine there. He had the idea of employing White Russians to work as guards at the mine and asked Colonel Yasue to act as a go-between. The date was not specified, but considering that the topic of Sugihara's issuance of visas in Kaunas came up and that Yasue was dismissed from his office immediately after the signing of the Tripartite Pact on September 27, 1940, it must have been during that September.

Yasue told Furusaki that Jews were being persecuted in Germany, a fact not made public in Japan at the time, and explained that most of the White Russians resident in Manchuria were Jewish. He also divulged the little-known story that he had played a part in the rescue of around two hundred Jewish children who had sought help at the Japanese embassy in Warsaw after the German army invaded Poland. In the same vein, he mentioned that the Japanese consul in Lithuania had disregarded the objection of the Foreign Ministry and issued visas, rescuing around one thousand Jews who then fled to Manchuria. As would have been expected, word of Sugihara's activities had quickly reached the ears of the greatest expert in Jewish matters in the Japanese army. Yasue added, "Sadly, that consul was reprimanded by the Ministry and it looks as if he is being recalled to Japan." What was behind this clear misapprehension?

---

38 Furusaki Hiroshi, *Suigin to sensō* [Mercury and war] (privately published, Kinto, 1971).

At this same time, a report entitled "Concerning Restrictions on the Issuance of Visas to European Refugees" was sent from the Police Bureau of the Home Ministry to the head of the Bureau of American Affairs. It said that there had been an increase in the number of refugees from Europe as a result of the intensification of the war. Among them were those who had obtained Japanese transit visas on declaring their intention to acquire an entry permit to a third country after arrival in Japan but, once in Japan, had sought to obtain permanent residence there on the grounds that they had been unable to obtain an entry permit for the destination country. There were also those who had tickets to Japan, but no money to buy passage onward. There was a danger that these people would stay in Japan long term, and the Home Ministry was concerned about how to respond. It insisted that Japanese transit visas should only be issued to those possessing tickets to the destination country, sufficient funds, and entry permits already issued by the government of that country. Unless those conditions were fulfilled, they should on no account be issued.

The Home Ministry, too, was thus urging the strict enforcement of the immigration law, at a time when "Sugihara survivors" were already arriving in Japan on the visas he had issued. The Home Ministry was clearly at its wits' end as to how to deal with the increasing numbers of refugees staying on in Japan. In response, the Foreign Ministry again notified its diplomatic offices abroad to strictly enforce the requirements of the immigration law and, on September 30, 1940, sent a telegram to the Japanese embassy in the Soviet Union, where the possibility was highest that refugees from Europe would go to seek transit visas. Essentially it stipulated a new criterion: having sufficient travel funds had been an important condition for receiving a transit visa, but now the previously imprecise "sufficient" was defined as covering necessary travel expenses to the destination country and a minimum of 25 yen per person as spending money while in Japan. The ambiguous "sufficient" had now been made specific.

On October 10, around 140 diplomatic offices in Europe and North and South America, as well as eight Japanese shipping companies, including Nippon Yūsen (NYK Line), Ōsaka Shōsen (O.S.K. Line), Kokusai Kisen, and Nihonkai Kisen, were notified and stricter enforcement was put in place. These companies were, of course, unable to issue visas, but by giving the situation the widest publicity and conveying the policy to the shipping companies, which had ample opportunities to come into contact with the refugees, the government seemed to have hoped that appropriate action would be taken. Therefore, it would not be surprising if, in the midst of the government's attempts to enforce strict adherence to the law, some people thought that the person responsible for the confusion—the consul in Kaunas—would be punished for his actions. This may be what was behind the rumor that he was going to be recalled, mentioned by Yasue. Though Yasue sympathized with the Jewish refugees, he probably saw this outcome as unavoidable given the ruckus that Sugihara's wholesale issuance of transit visas had caused. As it turned out, however, the times called for Sugihara's talents as an intelligence officer, and he received no kind of reprimand or punishment at all.

The Second Visa List

Sugihara served in Prague for less than six months, from September 1940 to February 1941. Perhaps because of the brevity of his posting there, very little research has been conducted on his time in Prague, but he continued to issue visas to Jewish refugees there as well. Two Visa Lists he compiled here are extant. Compared with the number of visas issued in Kaunas, there are very few names on these lists, and this may be why so little attention has so far been given them.

The first list was attached to regular official correspondence No. 17 dated February 4, 1941 from Sugihara, acting consul-general in Prague, to Foreign Minister Matsuoka Yōsuke. It

The Second (Prague) Visa List.
(Diplomatic Archives of the Ministry of Foreign Affairs, Japan)

gives the names of a total of eighty people who received visas: 73 between January 1940 and the end of the year and seven in January 1941. I will call this Sugihara's Second Visa List. Listed as "German (Jewish)" in the nationality column are 72 names, around 90 percent of the total. Of these, 42 were issued visas after Sugihara took up his appointment in Prague on September 10, 1940, 37 of them being Jews, again close to 90 percent.

Incidentally, there is no mention of "Jewish" in the nationality column of Kaunas Visa List. The majority of those who received visas in Kaunas were Polish Jews. Passports issued by the Polish government made no distinction between Jews and non-Jews. However, such a distinction does appear in the Second Visa List from Prague. The German government, preaching the exclusion of Jews, stamped passports of German Jews with a spiteful red "J." This resulted in "Jewish" being included in the nationality column of the Prague List.

A further point of difference between the two lists is that a column for "destination" appears in the Second Visa List. This would have been inserted by Sugihara's predecessor as consul-general, Ichige Kōzō,[39] and Sugihara followed suit. In addition, since the number of visas issued was comparatively few, there would have been sufficient time to confirm and enter the destinations.

The destinations in the Second Visa List, which contains visas issued by Ichige as well as Sugihara, are largely divided between the United States (16) and Central and South America (Brazil, Uruguay, Mexico, Honduras, Argentina, and Ecuador) (31). By the end of 1940, destinations were almost all limited to Shanghai. In the third list I will discuss below, all the German Jews had Shanghai as their destination. This indicates that, although the countries of Central and South America readily accepted Jewish refugees at first, those doors were gradually closed until only Shanghai remained as a destination.

In 1941, refugees who had been granted Japanese transit visas to countries in Central and South America were occasionally being refused the right

---

39 A South American expert who served as consul-general in São Paulo and was appointed as consul-general in Prague when the legation there was downgraded to consulate-general in June 1939.

to enter, and Japan had to respond to this situation. It therefore adopted a policy requiring refugees' passports to be checked again in Vladivostok and denied passage to Japan for those whose destinations were Central or South America. Nei Saburō, the acting consul-general in Vladivostok at the time, was actually eager to help the refugees out of their difficulties by issuing transit visas. He had been a younger classmate of Sugihara's at the School of the Japan-Russia Association in Harbin. He strongly asserted that forbidding transit through Japan just because the destination country was in Central or South America would cause a loss of confidence in Japan's transit visas. His view was not shared by the Ministry, but he was one of a number of Japanese diplomats who sympathized with refugees in this situation.

Compared with regular visa lists, the Second Visa List was handled by the Ministry in a slightly peculiar way. Such lists, including the one for the Kaunas consulate, were filed under the classification "Reports from Diplomatic Offices Abroad Regarding Foreigners' Passports and Visas." However, the Second Visa List (Prague) was filed under "Ethnic and Racial Problems" in the section related to Jewish people. Why was the Second Visa List treated differently from the Kaunas List and the Third Visa List discussed below, which was classified under passports and visas like the Kaunas List?

There is every likelihood this was the result of a mix-up. On February 4, 1941, the Ministry sent Sugihara a telegram asking him to report the number of Jewish refugees who had received visas in Kaunas. Since Sugihara sent a report concerning visas issued in Prague the same day (official correspondence No. 17), this list may have been improperly filed in place of the requested report.

Compared with telegrams, official correspondence took a considerable amount of time to arrive at the Ministry. The correspondence in question, No. 17, was received sometime in early March. It is filed after Telegram No. 10 from Foreign Minister Matsuoka to Sugihara (February 4, 1941) and Telegram No. 12 from Sugihara to Matsuoka (February 5, 1941). Telegram No. 10, as we have seen, required Sugihara to respond immediately by telegram concerning the number of Jewish refugees who had received visas during his time in Kaunas and ordered him to send the report by mail. The Second Visa List (Prague), in which 90 percent of the visas were issued to Jewish Germans, was attached to official correspondence No. 17 from Sugihara, with the same date as Telegram No. 10, and was probably mistakenly assumed to be the list referred to in the exchange of telegrams above and filed accordingly.

When studying the Second and Third Visa Lists, the most important point is whether or not visa applicants had satisfied the conditions for issuance. If visas were issued only to those who had done so, there would have been no problems, and the issuance would have followed normal consular procedures. Did Sugihara then observe the regulations in Prague?

The Stoessinger Family

The major reason that details of Sugihara's issuance of visas in Prague are shrouded in mystery is that, in addition to the fact that no documentary sources other than the Second Visa List have been found, almost no testimony exists from those who actually received the visas. There is, however, one such witness: Professor John Stoessinger, the famous American international political scientist.

Stoessinger was born into a Jewish family in Austria in 1927 and was thirteen when he received a visa from Sugihara in Prague. Let us trace his flight as described in a postscript to his book *Why Nations Go to War* and in a speech given on November 8, 2001, at the Holocaust Education Center in Fukuyama, Hiroshima Prefecture.

Soon after Germany annexed Austria in March 1938, John and his mother, who had been living in Vienna, fled to Prague, fearing for their lives. Czechoslovakia had become independent after the First World War and had built a country that thrived both democratically and economically under the leadership of its president, Tomáš Masaryk, the "father of the nation." It was a "Jewish paradise," where Jews had exactly the same rights as all Czechs.

For a while, they were able to settle down and breathe easier, but Czechoslovakia soon fell into Germany's clutches too. Six months after the *Anschluss* in Austria, Hitler demanded the cession of Sudetenland; it passed into German hands after the Munich Conference, even though the Czech government had not been consulted. Edvard Beneš, who had long served as foreign minister under Masaryk and succeeded him as president when he retired for health reasons in 1935, resigned on realizing Czechoslovakia had been abandoned by the world, and went into exile in England in October 1938.

On March 14, 1939, at Hitler's instigation, Slovakia declared independence and became a client state of Nazi Germany. The same day, Hitler called the Czech president Emil Hacha to Berlin, threatened him all night, and the following morning succeeded in getting him to sign a document entrusting the fate of the Czech people to the Führer (himself). The country was then partitioned. The territory remaining after the cession of Sudetenland and the independence of Slovakia became the Protectorate of Bohemia and Moravia and was subsumed into German rule.

Prague was no longer safe, and persecution of Jews began, just as it had in Germany and Austria, so the Stoessingers began visiting foreign consulates in the city seeking visas. Getting a visa became increasingly difficult after war broke out in September 1939. It was in January 1941 that they were finally granted a visa for Shanghai by the Chinese consul, but they had to pay "landing money," far in excess of the usual fee. Having at last obtained a visa, they went to Moscow seeking a transit visa across the Soviet Union. There they were told they would need to present a Japanese transit visa as a guarantee they could leave the Soviet Union. Since there was an economic advantage for the Soviets to have these refugees buy tickets on the Trans-Siberian using hard currency, they were quite eager to issue transit visas, but a Japanese transit visa was required to ensure they would not remain in the Soviet Union for a long period. Discouraged, the Stoessingers returned to Prague, but then the news spread that the new Japanese consul (actually, acting consul) was issuing Japanese transit visas even to those without a destination. They hastened to the consulate to discover they had to wait in line several days. When their turn came, they entered the office to be greeted, of course, by Sugihara, who appeared to the young John to be about thirty years old (he was in fact then forty-one). He patted the boy on the head and asked him in German if he spoke any Japanese. John had heard the word for "yes" by chance, and managed to reply, "*hai*." Smiling, Sugihara promptly handed the family their visas. This enabled them to procure a Soviet transit visa a few days later, and they left Prague on March 4, 1941, eventually arriving in Shanghai by way of Japan. They remained safely there during the Pacific War, and went to the United States afterward.

The Terezín ghetto.

Six months later, in September 1941, Reinhard Heydrich, known to be the second most powerful member of the SS, was appointed Acting Reich Protector of Bohemia and Moravia. He was one of the main architects of the Final Solution, the extermination of all Jews, and on his appointment declared that there would not be one Jew remaining in the protectorate by the end of the year. In 1942, a ghetto, mainly for Jews, was established in Terezín (German: Theresienstadt) about forty miles north of Prague, with the rebuilding of the old fortress there. A total of around 140,000 Jews were imprisoned there through the end of the war and subjected to forced labor; if too weak to work, they were transported to Auschwitz and murdered. It was said that if Auschwitz was Hell, Terezín was its waiting room. When Terezín was liberated following the German defeat, no more than 17,000 Jews remained alive; the rest had died either there or at Auschwitz. Over 15,000 children were taken away from their parents in the Terezín ghetto; most did not survive the forced labor. If Sugihara had not been consul in Prague, John Stoessinger would have been among the victims.

The Third List

The story of the Stoessinger family is fascinating in itself as an episode about one family's courageous and successful escape from the horrors of the Holocaust, but it is also important for the way it provides us a very revealing glimpse of Sugihara's visa issuance in Prague that attests to the audacity of Sugihara's actions behind the Third Visa List.

Let me first give an outline of this list. It contains the names of 37 people who were issued visas between the beginning of 1941 and the end of February the same year, when Sugihara was transferred to Königsberg. The first seven names on the list are duplicates of those on the Second List. Other than a visa granted to a diplomat taking up a post in Japan, the other 29 were German Jews issued transit visas with their final destination as Shanghai.

Nos. 12 and 13 on this list are Oskar and Irene Stoessinger. No. 14 is Hans Hirschfeld, the birth name of John Stoessinger. I assumed Nos. 12 and 13 were John Stoessinger's parents and wrote to him to check. "Indeed they are," he wrote in reply. "Mr. Sugihara saved us." This is proof of the trustworthiness of Professor Stoessinger's account and his lecture in Japan. Yet we remain confronted with a number of questions.

First, why did Sugihara attach a detailed visa report only to the Third Visa List and not to the First or Second? Let us first look at the content of the visa report that Sugihara called "Declaration of Alien Entering Japan," before examining its implications below. Items listed in the Declaration were:

1. Passport: (a. Issuing Authorities; b. Date of issue; c. Number; d. Date of Visa)
2. Name:
3. Nationality:
4. Residence:
5. Place of Birth:
6. Date of Birth:
7. Former Status or Occupation:
8. Present Status or Occupation:
9. Names and Addresses of: (a. Father; b. Mother; c. Wife; d. Husband)
10. Purpose of visit:
11. Anticipated Dates of Arrival in and Departure from Japan: / Prospective Period of Stay in Japan/
12. Place of Embarkation and Name of Vessel:
13. Expected Ports of Arrival and Departure in Japan:
14. Probable Place of Residence or Stay in Japan:
15. Names and Addresses of Acquaintances in Japan
16. Name and Occupation of Guarantor / if any / for the Visa:
17. Remarks:

Note:
1. If accompanied by persons of less than 16 years of age, their names and relationship are to be entered in the "Remarks" paragraph.
2. Any change which may occur after the filling of this declaration concerning matters in paragraphs 10–14, inclusive, is to be at once communicated to this office.
3. Fill out this form in English or in Russian.

It was also a requirement to attach a photo and to sign the form.

So why was this kind of detailed form attached only to the Third Visa List and not to the second? As mentioned previously, the first seven names in the third list are duplicates from the second list, which means their date of issue had to be before February 4, when the second list was sent. The person given serial number 8, the first new name in the Third Visa List, received a visa on February 6.

One possible explanation is that Sugihara, receiving Telegram No. 10 from the Ministry on February 4 and sensing that the Ministry had raised its guard over the issuing of visas to Jews, prepared the form to emphasize that he was observing the regulations to the letter. He had just sent the second list, in which ninety percent of visa recipients were Jews, when he received the telegram, and it is therefore very possible he wanted to appear to be acting strictly in accordance with regulations.

Did he, in fact, adhere to the regulations in Prague, unlike in Kaunas? There was no problem with issuing visas to people, Jews and non-Jews alike, who had entry permits for their destination countries and sufficient funds to support them on their journeys. Taking into consideration the fact that only a small number of visas were issued in Prague, it would be perfectly reasonable to assume that the applicants were issued visas because they complied with the rules and therefore presented no particular problem. In this case, issuing visas would have been within the scope of regular consular business.

To be honest, I believed this to be the logical conclusion until I read Professor Stoessinger's various recollections. Having done so, however, I found this theory to be inconsistent with Stoessinger's description of people trapped with nowhere to go, including Jewish refugees, flocking to the Japanese consulate-general when they heard the new consul was issuing Japanese transit visas, and his statement that when they arrived, they found a long line of people waiting and had to wait themselves for several days.

Rescuing Jews from the Hands of the Nazis

There was no reason for Professor Stoessinger to exaggerate Sugihara's achievements. He was thirteen, and the dangerous situation he and his parents were in must have sharply engraved the events of that time in his memory, so there seems little possibility that he would make any great error. Based on the premise that his testimony is true, I would like to attempt an interpretation.

My hypothesis is that, even in Prague, Sugihara continued to issue visas to Jewish refugees who did not meet the conditions. In Kaunas, refugees were primarily Polish, and when the Soviet Union annexed Lithuania, they flooded to the consulate seeking visas. As a result, a vast number were issued in a short time, and because they were so conspicuous, they attracted the attention of the Ministry. The situation in Prague was very different. When Sugihara arrived in September 1940, Czechoslovakia had already been partitioned for eighteen months. The menace of the Nazis permeated every corner of society, and most of those who had the resources to leave the country and felt their lives in danger had likely already made their escape.

Professor Stoessinger's maternal grandparents, who lived in Prague, were not swayed by his stepfather's impassioned pleas for them to leave and, optimistic that things in Prague would not get worse, remained. They were later taken to the Terezín Ghetto; no one knows what happened to them. There were three types of people in Prague. The first was like the Stoessinger family, who wanted to leave the country and had the means to do so. The second wanted to leave but did not have the funds. The third had not thought at all about leaving. Sugihara gave visas to applicants from the first group and entered their names in the visa list as per normal consular business. However, I suspect that he also gave visas secretly to applicants from the second group but did not enter their names in the list. If this were so, it would tally with Stoessinger's description of the large numbers of people waiting outside the consulate-general.

I suggest that it was specifically because Sugihara realized he had to act in a more prudent way after he received Telegram No. 10 of February 4 that he compiled the visa report from the application forms only of those who met the visa requirements.

Why was Telegram No. 10 sent? What bothered the Ministry was not the issuance of new visas, but the large number of refugees staying in Vladivostok. The telegram had been drafted by the Third Section of the Bureau of American Affairs, which was responsible for visas and passports, and passed on to be signed by the head the First Section of the Bureau of European and West-Asiatic Affairs, which had purview over the Soviet Union. If the problem had been about the issuance of new visas, surely it would have been passed on to the head of the Second Section, which was in charge of Germany and other European countries, excluding the Soviet Union. In light of this, Sugihara's act of attaching the aforementioned Visa Declaration Forms to the Visa List could be seen as something of an overreaction. Yet, considering that the telegram had expressly asked him to specify the number of Jewish refugees who had been issued visas in Kaunas, he may have felt that he had to be ultra-careful.

In any case, Sugihara's audacity in continuing to issue visas in Prague, under the domination of Nazi Germany, merits our admiration. As we have already seen, the visas he issued in Kaunas primarily rescued refugees from the hands of the Soviet Union. Those issued in Prague, by contrast, saved Jews from the Nazis.

According to Sugihara Yukiko's reminiscences, the foreign diplomats in Prague, including her husband, were gathered together and told by German Foreign Minister von Ribbentrop that their presence in Prague was inconvenient for Germany, and he ordered them in no uncertain terms to leave immediately. Amid the silence around him, Sugihara calmly stood up, looked squarely at von Ribbentrop, and said, "Germany cannot just order us to leave. Please explain your reasons." Sugihara later told her it was an intimidating atmosphere, typical of the Nazis. Von Ribbentrop was seated imposingly in a chair, behind which hung a photograph of Hitler. A savage-looking German Shepherd was tied up at the entrance to the room, and gave the impression that it would spring to the attack at the slightest signal. Where did Sugihara find the courage to stand up to von Ribbentrop, a man deeply trusted by Hitler at a time when Nazi power was at its peak?

Sugihara recounted this story to his wife in the highest of spirits, and she, too, was delighted by it. This episode attests to Sugihara's out-and-out antipathy to Nazism. Like his work in Kaunas, his activities in Prague are deserving of record.

I would like to end this chapter by mentioning that the Japanese legation in Sweden and the consulate-general in Vienna were also issuing visas to Jewish refugees at this same time, and there is no evidence that this became particularly problematic. The historical record does not tell us clearly if they were issued according to the regulations or not. But what is certain is that, even after the signing of the Tripartite Pact in September 1940, Japanese policy toward the Jews did not fundamentally change. The Pact did not kindle anti-Jewish discrimination in Japan.

CHAPTER EIGHT

The True Value of
an Outstanding Diplomat

To the Front Line of Soviet Intelligence Gathering

Why had Prague been chosen as Sugihara's next posting after Kaunas, the visa question ignored? An extremely interesting telegram survives which sheds light on the situation at this time. This is telegram No. 254, sent to Foreign Minister Matsuoka on July 31, 1940, just before the Soviet annexation of the Baltic states, by Ōtaka Shōjirō, the minister to Latvia, Estonia, and Lithuania and representative of all Japanese diplomats in the Baltic states.

Touching on the impending closure of all Japanese missions in the Baltic states, Ōtaka spoke of where Sugihara's next assignment should be. Ōtaka had visited Klaipėda, now ceded to Germany, to inspect it as the possible site for a new Japanese consulate in place of Kaunas. The suggestion had been made no doubt because, with Lithuania soon to become part of the Soviet Union, Klaipėda was now the nearest territory to it. However, his inspection had convinced him that it was not suitable for the consulate. If intelligence gathering was to be Sugihara's main task at the new consulate, Klaipėda, having been Lithuanian territory until very recently, was at an undeniable disadvantage due to the closure of foreign consulates, since diplomatic contacts themselves are very effective at gathering intelligence.

According to a report by Ambassador Kurusu at the end of August 1940, many countries were considering setting up consulates in Königsberg (Kaliningrad) in East Prussia. By March the following year, when Sugihara moved there, a great number of diplomatic offices had already been established, including, according to Sugihara Yukiko in her memoirs, the consulate-general of the United States. This further underscores why Klaipėda had not been considered suitable.

Ōtaka, too, regarded Königsberg as more suitable for a Japanese diplomatic office, but he was uneasy about Sugihara being the only official appointed there. If just the Russian-speaking specialist Sugihara were sent there, it would be immediately obvious that his main function was to gather intelligence on the Soviet Union. And since relations between Germany and the Soviet Union were still amicable, it would be hard for Germany to permit the opening of a consulate-general with that purpose. There was also the danger that the Soviet Union might protest to Germany. It would therefore be preferable to appoint another person, such as a German specialist, as the official consul-general, under whom Sugihara would carry out his intelligence activities vis-à-vis the Soviet Union. This would be easier for Germany to accept and less likely to ruffle Soviet feathers. If the establishment of a consulate/consulate-general in Königsberg were not possible, or if it were delayed, Sugihara could be transferred temporarily to Prague. At that time, there were no Japanese consulates in the former Polish territory occupied by Germany. However, if conditions were to change, and it became possible to open an office there, it would also be beneficial to send Sugihara there. Sugihara's provisional Prague posting seems to have taken his relationship with Polish intelligence into account. Ōtaka's telegram clearly reveals how diplomats on the ground made every effort to send Sugihara to the front line of the Soviet intelligence war. Tapped as one of a group of experts at the time of the Nomonhan Incident, Sugihara had been playing in the reserves, but now he had matured to be one of the very best players and had become an essential figure as far as Japanese diplomacy was concerned.

This is also apparent from Ambassador Kurusu's frequent telegrams concerning the opening of the Königsberg consulate-general. On August 29, 1940, with the closing of all diplomatic offices in the Baltic countries, he sent a telegram to the Ministry stating his opinion that the consulate-general should be set up in Königsberg. The official reason was that it was the political and economic center of eastern Germany and the starting point for the transport of goods from Europe to Japan by way of Siberia. He also pointed out it was an ideal place to gather intelligence concerning the status of Soviet-German relations, which was, of course, the real reason. A telegram he sent on October 17 again strongly recommended a consulate-general be opened as quickly as possible in Königsberg, an important site to obtain intelligence on Soviet-German relations now that the diplomatic offices in Warsaw, Kaunas, Riga, and Tallinn had had to close.

Kurusu also actively pushed for Sugihara's appointment to the new consulate-general. A telegram of November 2 began with a comment that intelligence about the Soviet Union should be obtained continuously and relentlessly. The expression "relentlessly" (*shitsuyō ni*) is rarely found in diplomatic correspondence and is a measure of Kurusu's great enthusiasm for the subject. He also put great import on the intelligence network Sugihara had built up, remarking that even its temporary suspension was "regrettable." He received permission from the Ministry to dispatch Sugihara to Königsberg even before the consulate-general opened.

What was the relationship between Sugihara's intelligence network and its links to Polish intelligence after Kaunas? One of the two officers associated with Sugihara there, Lieutenant Stanisław Daszkiewicz, escaped to Stockholm, the main base for the Polish intelligence service, after seeing off the Sugihara family on their way to Berlin by train. In Stockholm, his superior, from whom he sought orders of how to proceed, was none other than Major Michał Rybikowski, who had also escaped to Sweden using a Manchurian passport obtained for him through Sugihara and Onouchi, the military attaché.

Amazingly, Polish intelligence had obtained information quite early on about the visit of Soviet Foreign Minister Molotov to Berlin in November 1940 and the excessive demands that he made of Hitler and von Ribbentrop. Knowing that these demands had incurred Hitler's wrath, they predicted that war would break out between the two nations in the near future and instructed Daszkiewicz to continue to work with Sugihara. The two men worked together in Prague and later went together to Königsberg. Since both places were under German occupation, it goes without saying that they were considerably more dangerous for Daszkiewicz than independent Lithuania had been. It would have been inconceivable for Daszkiewicz to have accompanied Sugihara, or for Sugihara, knowing the danger, to have taken him on if there weren't deep bonds of trust between the two men.

The Königsberg consulate-general opened in March 1941. Germany had been slow to give permission even though the two countries were allied. Its reluctance had to do with Hitler's strict orders not to let Japan find out about the planned attack on the Soviet Union—codenamed Operation

Barbarossa—for which preparations were then secretly underway. A little under four months before the invasion started on June 22, Sugihara's new war began.

Intelligence about the Commencement of German-Soviet Hostilities

Königsberg, where Sugihara was appointed acting consul-general, was the largest city in East Prussia. It has twice experienced the strange fate of being a detached territory. First, after the First World War, it was separated from the main part of Germany by the Polish Corridor and the free city of Danzig, while after the Second World War, it was annexed by the Soviet Union and renamed Kaliningrad. Today it is an exclave of the Russian Federation, following the dissolution of the Soviet Union in 1991 and the independence of the Baltic states, and remains a thorn in relations between Russia and Lithuania. The great philosopher Immanuel Kant spent most of his life in Königsberg and died there. Sugihara Yukiko described it as "a small city mainly populated by Germans, a quiet place where the university at which the philosopher Kant studied is situated."

Daszkiewicz/Perz accompanied Sugihara to Königsberg and continued to work with him. His 1948 memoirs vividly portray his persistence in acquiring intelligence, whatever the danger.[40] In the middle of May 1941, Sugihara, Daszkiewicz, and Consulate Secretary Satō Tetsumatsu traveled to Klaipėda by car to observe the German military situation. It was a dangerous journey, with cars driven by Germans often tailing them. They drove along the border area, spying out petrol depots and tanks in the forest, numerous sentry posts, and no-entry signs even on paved roads leading into the forest. Daszkiewicz noted that, during the evening, Sugihara and Satō hurriedly coded a telegram to be sent in the morning; this is thought to be Telegram No. 8, sent on May 9. It contains truly astounding information. Sugihara had observed military train transports of about ten cars heading for Königsberg from Berlin every day and noted that rumors were circulating among German soldiers stationed in and around Königsberg that some

---

40 L. Daskiewicz, *Placówka wywiadowcza "G". Sprawozdania i dokumenta* [Intelligence outpost G. Reports and documents] (London, 1948).

decision concerning Soviet-German relations could be expected in June, given there were already as many troops in the area as in former Polish territory now occupied by Germany. German officers had been ordered to learn enough Russian to read maps, with Germans and White Russians (Tsarist émigrés) living in the Baltic region in great demand as Russian teachers. Around a dozen vessels, including one of the 30,000-ton class, had been standing by for more than a month in the East Prussian port of Pillau, and German tanks had been clattering along roads leading to Lithuania for several days. A Soviet tank battalion had also been deployed, and both sides were facing each other across the border. The telegram gives a detailed report of the situation just prior to the outbreak of war and makes the accurate prediction that it would begin "in June."

Telegram No. 8, concerning German preparations for war against the Soviet Union. (Diplomatic Archives of the Ministry of Foreign Affairs, Japan)

What was the perception of the Japanese embassies in Germany and the Soviet Union, for whom monitoring the situation was a major responsibility? Unfortunately, I have only been able to find one related telegram from each sent in May, but they both give a good picture of how accurately those embassies assessed the situation and provide an interesting comparison for Sugihara's telegram.

Telegram No. 556 from the embassy in Berlin was sent on May 17 by the pro-German General Ōshima Hiroshi, who had succeeded Kurusu Saburō in February 1941. Ōshima's telegram was based on information obtained by Embassy Counselor Kase Shun'ichi from a well-informed member of the legation of a certain country. As third-hand information, this was not nearly as trustworthy as the field intelligence gathered by Sugihara. The telegram reported that Stalin had asked Hitler to withdraw German troops from the border, saying that he would increase the amount of grain, oil, and other goods shipped to Germany by thirty percent in return. Germany was not satisfied by this and demanded greater amounts of mineral resources and foodstuffs. If war broke out between the two countries, the Soviet Union was at a clear disadvantage since Germany was already fully prepared. Stalin was, therefore, trying to convince his countrymen that the country needed to make whatever concessions it could to avert war. The telegram noted that Germany was seeking supplies from the Soviet Union only to continue the war against Britain and would likely resort to war only if the Soviet Union refused to give them this material support. Germany's utmost priority was the surrender of Britain, and it would only embark on war if Russia did not assist in this aim.

Telegram No. 596 was sent from the embassy in Moscow on May 16 by Ambassador Tatekawa Yoshitsugu, a former army officer. He reported that there was a plausible rumor circulating that Germany would attack the Soviet Union in the near future, so he had sought an interview with Molotov. Based on this meeting, he reported that, if there were a conflict between Germany and the Soviet Union at that moment, the Soviet Union would have no chance of winning, making Germany the one country that it was intent on not crossing swords with. Germany, for its part, needed to advance toward the Middle East to secure its supply of resources following its invasion of the Balkans in April 1941, so it absolutely wanted to avoid being obstructed by the Soviet Union. Ambassador Tatekawa had accordingly concluded that any war between Germany and the Soviet Union was inconceivable, and he conveyed this opinion in the telegram.

Why Did Sugihara Alone See the Possibility of War?

With historical hindsight it is easy to see that of the three telegrams, Sugihara's was the most accurate. Why was it that people in key positions like the ambassadors in Germany and the Soviet Union were fooled, while Sugihara alone had been able to obtain accurate intelligence?

In Ōshima's case, this was largely because the Germans had put a gag order on any mention of Operation Barbarossa to the Japanese. He was also known to be pro-German and was likely over-confident that Germany would not pull the wool over his eyes. We will discuss problems associated with Ōshima's reports further below.

Tatekawa's report simply detailed his interview with the Soviet foreign minister without any further assumptions. It is clear today that, at that time, Stalin obstinately believed that war with Germany was inconceivable. In the year leading up to the outbreak of hostilities, it is said that Stalin received over ninety reports warning of an attack by German forces. However, he did not take them seriously, probably because he believed that a leader like Hitler would not be so stupid as to instigate a war on two fronts, and therefore the Soviet Union would not be invaded while the war with Britain was still in progress. There is also reason to think that Stalin was left traumatized by the fact that the Soviet Union had not been invited to the Munich Conference in 1938, when the cession of Sudetenland had been decided, without its knowledge, by the four participating nations. He feared that at critical times, Britain and France would unhesitatingly concede to Germany, leaving the Soviet Union isolated.

Sugihara poked around some very dangerous places to dig up the kind of important intelligence that Ōshima and Tatekawa, in their elevated diplomatic roles, could not obtain. His provision of accurate information, right down to the time of the outbreak of war between Germany and the Soviet Union, was arguably the crowning achievement of his wartime career as an intelligence officer.

Nevertheless, however good the intelligence, it is meaningless if not acted upon. How important did the Foreign Ministry consider the information Sugihara sent? Foreign Minister Matsuoka sent a telegram to Ambassador Ōshima on May 28, ordering him to notify the German authorities that Japan did not want Germany to go to war against the Soviet Union, so there must have been some apprehension in Tokyo.

In any case, on June 3–4, Hitler received Ōshima at the Berghof, his chalet in Berchtesgaden, and informed him, in the presence of von Ribbentrop, that German-Soviet relations had soured and a military conflict was unavoidable. It was out in the open at last, but Hitler made no mention of when any action would occur. Ōshima sent this information in a telegram to the Ministry on June 5.

Though Sugihara had told the Ministry on May 9 that war would break out in June, there is no sign that any plans were made based on that intelligence. This is borne out by the fact that when reports came of the opening of hostilities on the fateful day of June 22, Matsuoka was attending a performance at the Kabukiza with Wang Jingwei, head of the Reorganized National Government in Nanjing (the Japan-backed puppet government created to oppose the Kuomintang government led by Chiang Kai-shek), who was then on a formal visit to Tokyo.

Yielding to German Pressure

As soon as he received the report of the German invasion, Matsuoka left the Kabukiza, changed his clothes, and went to the imperial palace. He appealed directly to the emperor for Japan to immediately declare war on Russia. This surprised the emperor, in view of the fact that the Soviet-Japanese Neutrality Pact had been signed just two months earlier, on April 13, and that Matsuoka himself, who had been one of the signatories, was now disregarding it and proposing war. When the emperor asked if the prime minster, Konoe Fumimaro, was of the same opinion, Matsuoka replied that he had not yet conferred with him, and he was told to go do so and then come back.

It is probable that Matsuoka had at last realized that the German attack on the Soviet Union was imminent when he received Ōshima's telegram of June 5, and had been mulling over how Japan should respond. But because he had not anticipated that it would happen so soon, he felt he did not have enough time at that point to sound out his cabinet colleagues, so took the emergency step of appealing directly to the emperor.

The emperor did not have a high opinion of Matsuoka, remarking to an aide on hearing Matsuoka's report of his visit to Moscow and Berlin in March and April of that year, "Has Matsuoka been bought by Hitler?" A recently discovered memorandum by the former head of the Imperial Household Agency, Tomita Tomohiko, reveals that on April 28, 1988, the emperor told Tomita of his strong displeasure that Class A war criminals (which includes those who died before final judgement)—above all Matsuoka and Shiratori Toshio (ambassador to Italy from 1938 to 1940)—had been enshrined at Yasukuni Shrine in 1978.

There were few who supported Matsuoka's idea of attacking the Soviet Union. But for all their opposition to a war with the Soviet Union,

"Guidelines for the Implementation of Imperial National Policy, including the Change of Circumstances" issued at the Imperial Conference on July 2, just over a week after the German attack, outlined a plan to take possession of European colonies in Southeast Asia, given what was as good as an "open door" provided by the capitulation of the countries of Europe to Germany. The northern part of French Indochina (Vietnam, Laos, and Cambodia) was already under Japanese occupation, and now the government decided to take the opportunity to advance into the south. This action was fiercely opposed by the United States, since it threatened American influence in the Philippines. The result was that Japanese assets in the United States were frozen and a total embargo was imposed on oil sales to Japan.

No doubt Sugihara kept abreast of news about the German army's onward push at this time, and he probably had questions about its ability to maintain its drive. He would have guessed that German momentum would weaken with the onset of winter, as the army moved into the vast territory of the Soviet Union. Now that the war had gone far beyond Königsberg—previously on the border between Germany and the Soviet Union—his circumstances no longer tested his intelligence skills, and time probably hung heavy on his hands.

On September 16, 1941, he put in a request to return to Japan, having already been in Europe for four years. He gave his son's education as a reason, also mentioning health concerns, and specifically asked if he could travel on the Nippon Yūsen liner, the *Asama Maru*, on its return voyage from Europe. Hiroki was indeed of school age, and Sugihara might have been concerned about the dangers of his family's continuing to be with him in a country at war, even if he was a diplomat. But he may have been motivated even more by the increasing difficulties he faced in operating as an intelligence officer. He was the subject of a memorandum from the Chief of the Sicherheitspolizei (SIPO, English: Security Police) to Hermann Göring in July 1941 that described him as "a friend of England and Poland."[41] A sense of personal danger may have prompted his application to hurriedly

---

41 Memo PIRA-1133, August 4, 1947, sent from Italy to Washington. Translation of a letter from the Chief of SIPO to Reichsmarshall Goering [*sic*], "Japanese Espionage in the Reich," dated July 1941.

return to Japan. There are now no documents to be found in the Foreign Ministry that tell us its reaction; however, on November 27, he was ordered to Romania as a first-class interpreter at the legation in Bucharest. He took up his duties there on December 10, two days after the Japanese attack on Pearl Harbor. What would his thoughts have been when he received the news that war had broken out?

A Country That Did Not Make the Most of Sugihara's Intelligence

It is not impossible, given what we know today, to surmise where Sugihara stood. The letter from the chief of SIPO to Göring gives details of his collaboration with Lieutenant Daszkiewicz/Perz and states "In his new position at the Consulate in Königsberg, Sugihara was so assiduous in his efforts for the I.S. [Intelligence Service] that his stay in Königsberg threatened to become too much of a burden for friendly relations between Germany and Japan."[42] Japan's ally Germany was wary of Sugihara's shrewdness and, in a sense, it was only natural they should have wanted to get rid of him. In response, the Ministry transferred him to faraway Romania. Why was such a talented man blithely sent to a place where he could not be expected to operate as an intelligence officer? Why could the Ministry not have chosen a location far from Germany's prying eyes, where he could better work for the good of Japan?

At the time, the former military attaché at the Latvian legation, Colonel Onodera Makoto, was working in Stockholm as the military attaché at the Japanese legation in Sweden, collaborating with the Polish Intelligence Service. If Sugihara had at least been sent to this neutral country, he could have found some way to put his skills to use. But perhaps the real reason was that Japan, then steering recklessly toward war with the United States, absolutely had to cooperate with Germany. For Japan to win, the only possible scenario was reliance on others, for Germany to take Britain and the Soviet Union, and the United States, becoming weary of war, to accept peace in Japan's favor. For this scenario, as shaky as walking a tightrope, to work out well, Japan could not risk making any personnel assignments that might be even slightly detrimental to Germany.

---

42 Ibid.

Another important factor may have been the personality of the Japanese ambassador in Berlin, Ōshima Hiroshi. As discussed above, he was one of the most pro-German people in the army. He had served as military attaché in Germany since 1934 and was instrumental in the signing of the Anti-Comintern Pact in November 1936. In recognition of his services, he was appointed ambassador to Germany in October 1938. He worked feverishly with Shiratori Toshio, the Japanese ambassador to Italy, to expand the Anti-Comintern Pact between Germany, Japan, and Italy into a military alliance in November 1937.

When Sugihara was appointed acting consul in Kaunas in July 1939, Ōshima was still the ambassador to Germany, and Sugihara was aware that his job was to provide Ōshima with intelligence concerning the Soviet Union. However, Ōshima was recalled following the signing of the German-Soviet Nonaggression Pact in August and the sudden consequent change in Japanese relations with Germany. He was succeeded by Kurusu Saburō.

Following the conclusion of the Tripartite Pact in September 1940, Ōshima was reappointed ambassador to Berlin in December, taking up his post the following February. Sugihara paid him a formal visit when taking up his position as acting consul-general in Königsberg. Ōshima told him he had high hopes for his Russian language capabilities, and said in a friendly way that they should drink together sometime. Of course, "drink" in this context also implied reporting any intelligence gathered, rather than just sharing a bottle or two. At this point, there is little sign of any bad feeling on a personal level toward Sugihara.

Ōshima, though, had a completely different personality from Kurusu. He made no effort to create the kind of environment that would make the best use of Sugihara's abilities. Rather than collecting detailed intelligence and pursuing intelligence activities, he preferred making elaborate plots more likely to be found in the pages of an adventure novel, such as the overthrow of the Afghan government or the assassination of Stalin. He was also blatantly pro-German, and during the war, his reports were so favorable to Germany that it was almost common knowledge in the military, not to mention the government, that Ōshima's intelligence could not be relied upon. In 1943, despite the hazardous wartime situation, the Special

Mission to Germany and Italy led by Major General Okamoto Kiyotomi was dispatched from Japan to make a first-hand study of the situation in Europe, since it was said that Ōshima's information could not be trusted.

For Ōshima, German wishes were paramount, and though he acknowledged Sugihara's ability, he could not have proactively stood up for him as long as Sugihara was sidelined by Germany. In the previously mentioned unfinished account he wrote late in life, Sugihara criticized the "thoughtless, irresponsible, reckless career officers who collaborated with the Nazis." Ōshima was certainly representative of them. It was Sugihara's tragedy that such a man stood in the position of ambassador to Germany and so controlled his fate.

The Activities of Sugihara's Protegés

When Sugihara was transferred to the legation in Romania, Daszkiewicz/ Perz left him, but links between the Polish Intelligence Service and Japan continued. An important figure in that Service, Michał Rybikowski/Peter Iwanow, escaped, as previously seen, to Sweden under the protection of Sugihara and Onouchi Hiroshi, the military attaché in Latvia. In January 1941, around the same time Onouchi was transferred to Helsinki as military attaché, Onodera Makoto, who had played an active role when he was working at the Latvian legation in extending its jurisdiction to Lithuania and Estonia, was appointed military attaché to the legation in Sweden. There was communication between Sugihara and Onodera through the Polish Intelligence Service. When Sugihara was at the Königsberg consulate-general, he managed to ascertain German troop movements with the help of Daszkiewicz, as we have seen. At that time, Daszkiewicz had hoped that the telegram reporting these developments would also be sent to Stockholm to reach Rybikowski. Sugihara replied that he had heard that relations between Onodera and Rybikowski were extremely friendly and assured him that the information would certainly be passed on.

In *Rokusennin no inochi no biza*, Sugihara Yukiko wrote that Onodera also helped Jewish people, and that he and Sugihara appeared to be kindred spirits, still exchanging letters after the war. There seems, however, to be some doubt about this statement. Sweden, where Onodera was based, remained neutral during the war, and Onodera was not involved with issues concerning Jews. It would be more accurate to say that the two men were working together, not in relation to the Jewish issue, but through the Polish Intelligence Service. As a topflight intelligence officer, Sugihara would not have spoken to his wife about such contacts, so it seems that Yukiko mistakenly ascribed their contacts as having to do with Jewish refugees.

Kasai Tadakazu, then a diplomat in the Manchukuo legation in Berlin, was very close to Sugihara, coming from Gifu and studying at the Harbin Institute like him. "Mr. Onodera was not a military type," he remembered, "and he had a flexible mind. That is why he got on well with Mr. Sugihara." The two intelligence officers, among the best in their field, appear to have had much in common. Kasai also said that both were aware that if Japan declared war against Britain and the United States, it would lose.

After Sugihara was sent to Romania, intelligence contacts between Poland and Japan continued through the connection between Onodera and Rybikowski. Nothing changed in this regard, even after the Pacific War began with the attack on Pearl Harbor and Japan became an ally of Poland's enemy, Germany.

Day in, day out, Germany increased pressure on the Swedish government over Rybikowski, ever a thorn in its side, and in January 1944, Sweden finally acquiesced to his deportation. Even Onodera was unable to protect him and could do no more than help him move to London. In recognition of what Onodera had done for him, Rybikowski promised to continue sending him reports from Britain.

Did the Yalta Intelligence Arrive?
After arriving in London, Rybikowski moved away from intelligence activities and resumed his regular military duties, joining the Polish army in Italy. Meanwhile, his subordinates followed his orders and continued sending reports to Onodera, despite the danger. Onodera's reports were an important news source for the Japanese when intelligence capabilities diminished toward the end of the war.

Since Onodera was a military attaché, his telegrams were sent to the General Staff. According to his wife, Yuriko, who worked with him, he burned all the files in his possession after the war ended.[43] Because all telegrams and documents that were held in Tokyo relating to military matters were also destroyed, no trace remains of Onodera's telegrams in surviving Japanese records. Ironically, records of some messages that were intercepted and decoded do remain in the National Archives and Records Administration (NARA) in Washington, D.C. What is considered the most important piece of intelligence that Onodera received from the Poles concerned the Yalta Conference of February 1945. There, Roosevelt, Churchill, and Stalin made plans for the end of the war and discussed the postwar world order. At the insistence of the Soviet Union, Poland would lose territory in the east but be compensated by land in the west from Germany. The Yalta Conference cast the self-interest of the great powers into sharp relief. Roosevelt, fearing a long, drawn-out war with Japan, strongly encouraged Stalin to declare war against it; Stalin agreed to do so "two or three months after Germany has surrendered." This was the worst possible scenario for Japan.

After the war, Onodera remembered receiving this intelligence from the Poles, and recognizing its importance, sending a telegram using the most complicated code available. It must have worked, because no record of this important information can be found among the archives of messages intercepted and decrypted by the Americans. Mrs. Onodera wrote in *Barutokai no hotori nite* that her husband wanted an early end to the war, possibly through a peace plan brokered by Sweden, so he sent this intelligence back to Japan "with a prayer in his heart."

Unfortunately, there is no evidence that this important information was ever discussed among the General Staff. Perhaps if it had been dealt with appropriately, Japan would not have spent its energy in futile negotiations for a peace brokered by the Soviet Union. We can only mourn the loss of a possible chance to avoid the dropping of the atomic bomb on Hiroshima on August 6, the declaration of war by the Soviet Union on August 8, and the dropping of the atomic bomb on Nagasaki on August 9.

---

43 Onodera Yuriko, *Baruto-kai no hotori nite: Bukan no tsuma no Daitōa sensō* [On the shores of the Baltic: The Greater East Asia War of a military attaché's wife] (Tokyo: K.K. Kyodo News, 1985).

EPILOGUE

Regrets of an Intelligence Officer

I have been studying Sugihara Chiune for more than thirty years, but there is one thing that puzzles me. When Sugihara was posted to Kaunas, Katayama Junnosuke, then a clerk at the legation in Latvia (and later ambassador to Liberia, 1973–1977), visited him there on business. He had heard that Sugihara was reputed to be an exceptional Russian linguist, yet found him a very likeable person who did not assume any air of seniority. That evening, though, Sugihara downed several glasses of alcohol in Katayama's presence and kept on muttering, "Why? Why? Even though I've done something no one else did, and have gone to such lengths…" This image of a man mumbling grievances over his drink does not at all correspond with the Sugihara Chiune I have been studying for so long.

If we look at Sugihara just as a humanitarian, we will never be able to understand the meaning of his lament. Only Sugihara himself knows, and what I am about to write is no more than a hypothesis. But when I look back over his life until then as an intelligence officer, I can't help wondering, "What if?" This type of grumbling generally has its origins in discontent with work—inadequate compensation for the job or a promotion slow to come, for instance. I have no intention of portraying Sugihara as a perfect person, and I don't think it's impossible that he felt the dissatisfaction that is an unavoidable part of being a salaried worker. All the same, I am curious about his saying, "I've done something no one else did." What was it that he had done to have given him this kind of pride?

Katayama visited Kaunas around March 1940, before the Soviet annexation of the Baltic states and before Jewish refugees began flocking to the Japanese consulate. What was Sugihara doing at that time? As we have seen, he had been selected as one of several specialists posted to Europe to gather Soviet intelligence, and in a short period of time, he had built up a collaborative relationship with the Polish intelligence service and was sending back valuable information. It was for that very reason that Ambassador Kurusu in Berlin and Ōtaka Shōjirō, the minister in Riga, worried about his next posting after the Kaunas consulate closed. If this kind of concern is a sign of their evaluation of his espionage efforts, then the root of his discontent might well have been of a different dimension to mundane worries over pay and promotion.

What is an intelligence officer's raison d'être? It is scarcely an exaggeration to say that it is to acquire valuable information and then have it interpreted correctly and acted upon. I cannot help thinking that what would have followed Sugihara's "Even though I've done something no one else did, and have gone to such lengths…" might well have been a lament of the order, "Why wasn't the intelligence I faced danger to acquire not used properly?"

It was just then that a man's face showing infinite regret came to mind, an expression full of an inexpressible and bitter disappointment and sadness. A documentary called *Nichi-bei kaisen fuka nari* (Japan and the United States must not go to war), broadcast by Japanese public broadcaster NHK in December 1985, contains an important interview with the former military attaché in Stockholm, Onodera Makoto, then still alive. I will never forget the expression on his face when he began speaking about the fact that the Japanese government did not act on telegrams he sent concerning the Yalta Conference. I had never before seen such pain on a person's face.

In my mind, Onodera's pained expression and Sugihara's lament correspond perfectly, speaking eloquently of the harsh realities of the intelligence world they were required to navigate, and also offering valuable hints as to how we should navigate the present-day world, inundated as it is with information. Intelligence is a matter of sifting through both overt and covert information to distill the wisdom required to shape the future. I would be very happy if this book serves, even if only minimally, to arouse its readers' interest in intelligence activities.

AFTERWORD

What happened to Sugihara after he gave up his career as an intelligence officer and left the Foreign Ministry? When he left government employment, he also moved away from intelligence activities, as far as we can tell. However, information that has recently become available suggests that he continued to make use of his superlative linguistic skills and the abilities he fostered during his time as an intelligence officer.

He retired from the Foreign Ministry in 1947, and had a variety of jobs afterward. In 1960, a few years after the resumption of Japanese-Soviet relations in 1956, he became manager of the Moscow branch of Kawakami Trading, and though he subsequently changed jobs several times, he remained in Moscow for fifteen years. He did not take his family with him.

It is curious that Sugihara continued to work for fifteen years in a country that had previously refused him a visa. His skill in Russian was, of course, beyond reproach. However, as we have seen, he was an accomplished linguist, fluent in a number of other languages. I am probably not alone in thinking that he didn't have to deliberately work in a country that had caused him so many difficulties in the past.

Watanabe Katsumasa[44] relates an interesting conversation between three men who had worked under Sugihara at the Moscow office of Kawakami

---

[44] Watanabe Katsumasa, *Sugihara Chiune no higeki* [The tragedy of Sugihara Chiune] (Tokyo: Taisho Shuppan, 2006).

Trading: Jinma Kikuya, Kawamura Suguru,[45] and Tamura Shunsuke. According to these men, Sugihara was a man of few words, like a samurai of old, and made no mention at all about issuing visas to Jewish refugees. But he also had a kindly side, full of humor, and was trusted by his subordinates. His Russian had not declined at all; in fact, it was so good that he would correct letters drafted by his Russian secretary.

A famous episode from his time at Kawakami Trading is when he translated the *norito* (Shinto ritual prayers) into Russian to be used at the launch of an oil tanker commissioned by the Soviet Union. The launching ceremonies of tankers built at Japanese shipyards were conducted according to Shinto rites, and involved the offering of *norito*. These are not easily understood even by Japanese, which made these ceremonies tedious occasions for Soviet attendees, from the ambassador on down. However, the launching ceremony Sugihara attended on one of his visits to Japan was completely different. He skillfully translated the *norito* into Russian on the spot, transmitting their purpose to the attendees, and apparently everyone was delighted.

The three former Kawakami employees agree that Sugihara knew exactly how to win the hearts of Russians, understanding their temperament very well. He seems to have made use of the skills he had cultivated as an intelligence officer to foster good relations between the Soviet Union and Japan in a time of peace. He continued to involve himself in various activities into his old age. I said in the Introduction that I hope the younger generation will read this book, but I would be doubly happy if it serves as encouragement for older readers as well. When I spoke with the actor Misawa Shingo, who has been playing Sugihara in a one-man play for more than ten years, he told me he would like to continue doing so until he reaches eighty-six, Sugihara's age at death. I am still in my fifties, with plenty of life before me, and those words resonated with me.

Even so, it has been a great challenge for me to assemble this portrait of Sugihara Chiune as an intelligence officer. When it was suggested that I

---

45 Kawamura Suguru, historian and translator, was the father of pop singer Kawamura Kaori, who died of breast cancer in 2009, at the early age of thirty-eight. Sugihara had been the matchmaker in his marriage to Elena Alexandrovna Skudnova in Moscow, as Kaori wrote in her book *Helter Skelter* (Tokyo: Takarajimasha, 2005).

write such a study, my expression must have resembled a mixture of surprise and bewilderment, like that of Charlie Chaplin's Barber toward the end of *The Great Dictator*, in the famous scene where he has been mistaken for the dictator Adenoid Hynkel (also played by Chaplin and based on Adolf Hitler) and has no choice but to deliver a public speech before a great crowd. Since my previous research had dealt with Sugihara as a humanitarian, I thought it would be too much for me, and my lips started to move on their own accord with the words of the Barber, "I'm sorry.… That's not my business." However, as I wrote in the Foreword, I strongly felt I needed to take a step further in my study of Sugihara and, following the lead given to me by Teshima Ryūichi, go beyond the topic of Sugihara the humanitarian. I decided to take on the task myself rather than leaving it up to someone else, and took the plunge. I leave the result to the judgment of my readers.

I wrote at the beginning of the first chapter that Sugihara's life was marked by fate and chance. These have also marked my own life through my study of Sugihara. The great watershed moment in my life occurred more than twenty-five years ago, when I came across *Rokusennin no inochi no biza* immediately after its publication. At the time, I was studying Japanese-Soviet relations around the time of the Manchurian Incident, but before I knew it, research into Sugihara became my life's work. As the saying goes, "Flirtation gets serious before you know it."

A very fond memory is my "discovery" of the document "Concerning the Contacts with White Russians of Interpreter (Official) Sugihara" that I have mentioned several times in this book. This important source that sheds light on Sugihara's early career lay sleeping undisturbed for over seventy years in the Ministry's archive. I think it was fate rather than chance that eventually led me to it while I was searching the archive, intent on finding any documents connected with the Soviet refusal to grant Sugihara a visa.

I cannot reach the heights of the Barber's final speech in *The Great Dictator*, which moves from initial hesitation to a glorious message of love for all people, but I would be delighted if this book contained a worthwhile message for those with an interest in Sugihara or in intelligence matters. It is the result of more than twenty-five years' research (flirtation?), during which time I have been supported by a great many people.

I have been privileged to have valuable conversations with Mrs. Sugihara Yukiko, and equally fortunate to have spoken directly with Dr. Kurihara Ken, the walking dictionary of the Foreign Ministry, concerning the impression Sugihara created during his time there and the state of the refugees who had fled from Europe. However, a great many people, including Mrs. Sugihara and Dr. Kurihara, passed away before they could see this book. They include my mentor, Professor Fujimura Michio, who encouraged me to delve as deep as I could, given the importance of the topic; my former teacher, Professor Hirose Shizuko, who told me she was looking forward to the book being completed; Associate Professor Takahashi Hidenao, who urged me when I was still in my twenties to keep going with my research and publish articles, even if I thought no one would read them, because someone would surely find them of value; the film director Kumai Kei, who told me he'd like to make a film about Sugihara; Kawamura Kaori; and my mother, Yoshie.

There is a series of novels that I like very much called *Tengoku no honya* (Heaven's bookstore), by Matsuhisa Atsushi and Tanaka Wataru. I would like to believe, just as portrayed in those books, that there is also a bookshop in Heaven where a mysterious store manager wearing a Hawaiian shirt will hand out copies of this book to all the people mentioned above, to join Sugihara Chiune in reading it. I think it will be some time before I am able to ask them what they think, but I look forward to hearing their thoughts at length someday.

I would like to express my special thanks to Teshima Ryūichi, mentioned above, a former bureau chief at the NHK Washington Bureau and professor in the Graduate School of Keio University. It was he who served as a major driving force behind this book by suggesting that it was high time to focus on Sugihara as an intelligence officer as well as an exemplary humanitarian.

I am grateful for all the help, both officially and personally, that I received from Hamaguchi Manabu, emeritus professor of Kokugakuin University, and from his son Hamaguchi Akira, who both scrupulously went over the contents of this book with me. Since my own background is in Japanese history, the guidance I received from Professor Hamaguchi in European diplomatic history was extremely valuable.

I have been greatly privileged to have had a close relationship with Mrs. Sugihara and members of the Sugihara family, and have received many suggestions concerning this book from them. I would like to express my deepest gratitude in particular to Mrs. Sugihara Michi, widow of Chiune's eldest son Hiroki, and to her eldest daughter, Madoka, granddaughter of Chiune. Mrs. Sugihara Michi's granddaughter Oriha is now closely involved in studying her great-grandfather's life. I hope that this book will prove to be of some use to her.

From the time I first reported on Sugihara Chiune at a seminar led by Miwa Kimitada, now emeritus professor at Sophia University, he has spurred me on to put the information together as quickly as possible. I have made him wait a long time, but I am delighted to be able to tell him that, at last, it has been organized in book form.

The work of Professor Ewa Pałasz-Rutkowska of Warsaw University in Poland elucidating the connections of Sugihara with the Poles has been of inestimable help to me. I remember fondly her guiding me and my wife around Warsaw when we visited the city on our honeymoon.

I would like to express my deep gratitude for the encouragement and insights I have received from Hara Yoshihisa, emeritus professor, Tokyo International University; Inaba Chiharu, professor, Meijō University; Ishii Osamu, emeritus professor, Hitotsubashi University; Maruyama Naoki, emeritus professor, Meiji Gakuin University; Nakami Tatsuo, professor, Tokyo University of Foreign Studies; Ogawa Tsuneko, formerly professor at Teikyo University; Seki Yukihiko, professor, Nihon University; Shima Sonoko, professor, Showa Women's University; Tajima Nobuo, professor, Seijo University; Tani Teruhiro, professor, Tsuruga Junior College; Tōmatsu Haruo, professor, National Defense Academy; and Yakov Zinberg, professor, Kokushikan University.

I would also like to acknowledge those I would never have met if Sugihara Chiune had not been my subject of research: Watanabe Katsumasa, president, Taisho Shuppan; Furue Takaharu, former director, Port of Humanity Tsuruga Museum; Inoue Osamu, a walking dictionary of Tsuruga history; Kunieda Taisaku, former director, Sugihara Chiune Memorial Hall, Yaotsu-chō, Gifu Prefecture; Rev. Ōtsuka Makoto, director, Holocaust Education

Center; Jufuku Shigeru, photographer, who has published collections of photos of places associated with Sugihara; Enomoto Tetsuya, journalist, former Shitamachi bureau chief, Tokyo Shimbun, author of many articles on the subject of Sugihara, including "Jiyū e no tōsō" (Flight to freedom); Ishioka Fumiko, representative, Tokyo Holocaust Education Resource Center, an institution dedicated to telling children about the history of the Holocaust; Satō Fumio, actor, Dora Theatrical Company, who portrayed Sugihara on stage for more than twenty years; the previously-mentioned Misawa Shingo, actor; and students belonging to the Chiune Bridging Project at Sugihara's alma mater, Waseda University. I can't help feeling that Sugihara Chiune guided me to all of these people.

Seki Eiji, the former Japanese ambassador to Hungary, who was a guest on the NHK series *Sono toki rekishi ga ugoita* (Moments that made history) in a program about Sugihara, is a veteran of research into Sugihara in the Foreign Ministry. Through his auspices, I was privileged to contribute an article when the monthly magazine *Rekishi kaidō* (History road) published a special issue devoted to Sugihara in March 2001, and I would also like to thank him for the many things he has taught me since then.

It was an undeserved honor to have been given the opportunity to visit Lithuania when I was invited to speak at a symposium commemorating the tenth anniversary of the opening of Sugihara House in Kaunas in May 2010. I would like to express my deep gratitude to H.E. Ms. Akashi Miyoko, ambassador to Lithuania, and members of her staff, including Seki Izumi, counselor; Tsunashima Haruhiro and Ogawa Tomoko, secretaries; and Yoshino Satomi, specialist researcher, who gave me tremendous support during my stay in the country.

I also thank from the bottom of my heart Simonas Dovidavičius, director of Sugihara House, and members of Vytautas Magnus University, including Professor Egidijus Aleksandravičius, Vice-Rector Dr. Linas Venclauskas, and Dr. Aurelius Zykas, head of the Centre for Asian Studies, who translated my lecture, and to all the students who listened so carefully. I pray that this book will contribute to the further deepening of good relations between Japan and Lithuania.

This book could not have reached completion without Satō Seiichirō, member of the editorial committee at my publisher, Shinchosha. I would like to take this opportunity to thank him for his guidance and suggestions, which have always been incisive, and the valuable hints he gave me when we met during our discussions. I very much hope that we will be able to work together again to describe the intelligence officers who operated before and during the war.

It has been the joy of my life that I have come to know more and more people through Sugihara Chiune, from the time this book first appeared in the Shinchosha sensho edition in 2011 until now. Sadly, I cannot thank them all by name due to limitations of space, but I am sure there will be opportunities in the future to pursue the subject of Sugihara Chiune.

Finally, my heartfelt thanks go to Hasegawa Mayu of the Shincho Bunko editorial department, whose efforts brought this pocket edition into being, despite the tight schedule (usually my fault) and the record-breaking heat wave.

Shiraishi Masaaki
August 2015

Timeline

Year	Sugihara Chiune	Japanese and World Events
1900	Birth (January 1)	Siege of foreign legations in Beijing (June 20); Boxer Rebellion (November 1899–September 1901) Introduction of legal requirement for military ministers' positions to be appointed from active duty officers
1901		Birth of Hirohito, future Japanese emperor of the Showa era (April 29)
1902		Signing of first Anglo-Japanese Alliance in London (January 30)
1904		Declaration of Russo-Japanese War (February 10)
1905		Treaty of Portsmouth (September 5)
1906		Japan-Russia Association founded
1907		Russo-Japanese Agreement (July 30)
1912	Enters No. 5 Aichi Prefectural Middle School (now Zuiryō High School) (April 1)	Death of the Meiji emperor (July 30); Taisho era begins
1913		Abolition of legal requirement for military ministers' positions to be appointed from active duty officers
1914		Assassination of Franz Ferdinand (June 28) Outbreak of First World War (July 28) Japan enters war allied to Entente Powers (August 23)
1915		Japan issues 21 Demands of China (January 18); Anti-Japanese demonstrations intensify
1917	Graduates from Middle School (March 26) Submits blank sheets in examination to medical college earning father's ire (June)	Russia: February Revolution (March 8), abdication of Tsar Nicholas II (March 15) October Revolution (November 7) [These dates are according to the Gregorian calendar]
1918	Enters English Department of Waseda University Higher Normal School (April)	President Wilson of the USA issues 14 Points for World Peace (January 8) Brest-Litovsk Treaty (March 3) Japanese Siberian intervention declared (August 2), triggering rice riots throughout Japan Armistice (November 11)

Year	Sugihara Chiune	Japanese and World Events
1919	Passes Foreign Ministry examination for language cadets (July 17) Appointed Foreign Ministry cadet (September 21)	May 4th Movement, China (May) Treaty of Versailles (June 28)
1920	"From Snowy Harbin" (April) Voluntary enlistment in army, temporary withdrawal from studies (November 16, to March 1922)	League of Nations founded (January 10) Annexation of Vilnius by Poland Nikolayevsk Incident (May 25) School of the Japan-Russia Association opened in Harbin (September)
1921	Death of mother Yatsu (August)	
1922	Completes army service (March 31) Resumes studies (September)	Unilateral withdrawal of Japanese troops from Siberia announced (June 24); completed October 25
1923	Moves to Manzhouli for study (March)	Great Kanto earthquake (September 1)
1924	Appointed Foreign Ministry consular clerk (*shokisei*) (February 8) Marriage registration to Klaudia Apollonova submitted (February 15) Appointed to the Harbin consulate-general (December 15), appointment taken up the following January Marriage approved (December 26)	
1925		Soviet-Japanese Basic Convention, Beijing (January 20); diplomatic relations resumed with U.S.S.R. Public Security Preservation Law (April 22) General Election Law (May 5) Locarno Pact (signed December 1)
1926		Zhang Zuolin captures Beijing (June) National Revolutionary Army under Chiang Kai-shek begins Northern Expedition (June) Death of the Taisho emperor (December 25), Showa era begins
1927	Ordered to Beijing to examine seized documents (April) "General Survey of the National Economy of the Soviet Union" distributed within Foreign Ministry (November)	NRA attack Nanjing (March) Zhang Zuolin adherents in Beijing raid Soviet embassy (April)
1928		Stalin's first Five Year Plan Crackdown against Communists in Japan (March 15) Assassination of Zhang Zuolin by the Kwantung Army (June 4)

Year	Sugihara Chiune	Japanese and World Events
1929		Mass arrests of Communists in Japan (April 16) Legation opened in Riga (September 1)
1931	Meeting with Ōhashi Chūichi	Ōhashi Chūichi appointed as consul-general, Harbin (June) Railway tracks blown up at Liutiaogou (September 18), the Manchurian Incident Resignation of the second Wakatsuki cabinet (December 11), inauguration of the Inukai cabinet
1932	Interpreter in talks with CER about using it to transport troops (February) Ōhashi Chūichi communicates to Foreign Minister Yoshizawa Kenkichi his wish to take Sugihara with him to the Manchurian Government Foreign Affairs Department (March 17) Appointed secretary to the Office of the Commissioner of the Manchurian Government Foreign Affairs Department (June 11) Drafts a rebuttal of the Lytton Report	Harbin taken by Kwantung Army (February 5) Proclamation of state of Manchukuo (March 1) Lytton Commission in Manchuria (spring) Assassination of Prime Minster Inukai (May 15) Lytton Report issued (October 2) Japanese rejection of nonaggression pact with the Soviet Union (December 13)
1933	First round of formal negotiations for the sale of the CER between the Soviet Union and Manchukuo (June 26) Negotiations suspended over the imprisonment of Soviet employees and the "Fictitious Documents Affair" (October)	Lytton Report adopted by the League of Nations (February 24) Formal notice of Japan's withdrawal from the League (March 27) Tanggu Truce between China and Japan (May 31)
1934	Resumption of the CER negotiations (February 26) Appointed director in the Manchukuo Foreign Affairs Department. Manager of the Russia Section and Head of the Planning Section (August 25)	Tentative trade agreement with Estonia (June 21) U.S.S.R. enters League of Nations (September 18)
1935	CER talks conclude (March 23) Resigns from the Manchukuo Foreign Affairs Department, returns to the Japanese Foreign Ministry (July 1) Divorce from Klaudia by mutual consent (December 30)	Germany announces its rearmament (March 16) British delegation to Berlin (March 25) Anthony Eden, Lord Privy Seal, visits Moscow (March 28–31) Nuremburg Laws enacted in Germany (September 15). Intensification of anti-Jewish measures

Year	Sugihara Chiune	Japanese and World Events
1936	Marriage with Kikuchi Yukiko (April 7) Interpreter for Japanese-Soviet fisheries negotiations, Petropavlovsk First son Hiroki born (September 20) Appointed second secretary-interpreter of embassy in Russia (December 26)	Onodera Makoto takes up position of military attaché in Latvia (January) Death of George V (January) 2.26 Incident (February 26). Martial law in Tokyo until February 29 Hirota Kōki forms government (March 9) Yoshida Shigeru takes up position as ambassador to Great Britain (June) Spanish Civil War breaks out (July 17) Legal requirement for military ministers' positions to be appointed from active duty officers reintroduced by Hirota cabinet Hitler's "Confidential Memo on Autarky" (August) Anti-Comintern Pact with Germany (November 25) The Foreign Ministry upgrades the Latvian legation to be responsible also for Estonia and Lithuania (December 23)
1937	Declared *persona non grata* by Benedict Kozlovsky, Director of the Second Eastern Department, and given notice of the refusal of an entry visa (February 4) Horinouchi Kensuke calls Nicolas Rayvid to the Ministry seeking positive action regarding the Sugihara issue; Rayvid points out Sugihara's involvement with White Russians in Harbin (February 23) Meeting in Moscow between Shigemitsu and Stomonyakov over the Sugihara affair; Russian attitude unchanged (February 28) Submission of report "Concerning the Contacts with White Russians of Interpreter (Official) Sugihara" (March) Appointed to the Japanese legation in Finland (August 12) Arrives in Helsinki (September 15)	Resignation of Hirota cabinet (January) Formation of Hayashi cabinet (February 2) Lists of visas issued required by Foreign Ministry (May 3) Marco Polo Bridge Incident (July 7), outbreak of conflict between Japan and China Sino-Soviet Nonaggression Pact (August 21) Anti-Comintern Pact signed in Rome between Germany, Japan, and Italy (November 6)

Year	Sugihara Chiune	Japanese and World Events
1938	Japanese ambassador in Paris, Sugimura Yōtarō, asks the Ministry for Sugihara to be transferred to Paris (March 4); denied Birth of second son Chiaki (October 29)	Germany annexes Austria [*Anschluss*] (March 13) Zhanggufeng Incident (July 29–August 11) Munich Agreement over Czechoslovakia (September 29); Germany acquires Sudetenland Kristallnacht in Germany (November 9), sudden increase in Jewish refugees
1939	Appointed vice-consul, ordered to transfer from Helsinki to Kaunas (Lithuania) as acting consul to open a consulate there (July 20) Arrival in Kaunas with family (August 28) Lease taken out for consulate office (October 7) Visits family of Solly Ganor (December)	Cabinet of Hiranuma Kiichirō (January) Czechoslovakia partitioned (March 14) Klaipėda ceded to Germany (March 22) Death of Sugimura Yōtarō (March 24) Outbreak of Nomonhan Incident (May 11) Five Ministers Conference requests Army Minister Itagaki Seishirō to resolve the Nomonhan Incident through diplomatic negotiations (July 17) Signing of the German-Soviet Nonaggression Pact [Ribbentrop-Molotov Treaty] (August 23) Resignation of Hiranuma Cabinet, saying the situation in Europe was complex (August 28) German attack on Poland (September 1) Great Britain and France declare war on Germany; outbreak of the Second World War (September 3) Japanese government declares its non-involvement in the European war (September 4) Nomonhan ceasefire (September 15) Soviet attack on Poland (September 17) German-Soviet Frontier Treaty (September 28) Soviet-Estonian Mutual Assistance Treaty (September 28) Soviet-Latvian Mutual Assistance Treaty (October 5) Soviet-Lithuanian Mutual Assistance Treaty (October 10) Vilnius returned to Lithuania (October 28) Soviet invasion of Finland (Winter War) (November 30) Soviet Union expelled from League of Nations (December 14)

Year	Sugihara Chiune	Japanese and World Events
1940	Report on Belarus (February 27) Visit of Katayama Junnosuke (around March) Birth of third son, Haruki (May 28) Refugees begin appearing at the consulate (July 18) Large-scale issue of visas begins (July 26) Kaunas Consulate closed (August 28) Stay at Hotel Metropolis Leaves Kaunas (September 4 or possibly 5) Arrives in Prague via Berlin as acting consul-general Prague (September 12)	Surrender of Finland to the Soviet Union (March 12) Fall of the Netherlands to Germany (May 15) Fall of Belgium to Germany (May 28) German army enters Paris (June 14) Soviet Union gives ultimatum to Lithuania (June 14); accepted the following day. Soviet troops enter Lithuania (June 16) Battle of Britain (July–October) Lithuania incorporated into the Soviet Union (August 3) Tripartite Pact (September 27) German-Soviet Axis talks (October–November)
1941	Kaunas Visa List sent from Prague (February 28) Leaves Prague (February) Posted to Königsberg to open new consulate-general (February 28) Arrives Königsberg (March 6) Reports German military buildup against Soviet Union (May 9) Requests Foreign Ministry by telegram permission to return to Japan (September 16) Ordered to Bucharest (Romania) as first-class secretary-interpreter at the legation (November 27) Arrives Bucharest (December 10)	Soviet-Japanese Neutrality Pact signed in Moscow (April 13) Germany begins attack of the Soviet Union (June 22) Germans occupy Lithuania (June) Outbreak of Pacific War (December 8)

List of Notable Persons

Abe Nobuyuki (1875–1953), army general, prime minister 1939–1940.

Adachi Kenzō (1864–1948), home minister (Minseitō) 1929–1931.

Amakasu Masahiko (1891–1945), a former lieutenant in the military police, sent to Harbin by the Kwantung Army to organize anti-Japanese actions there.

Amō Eiji (1887–1968), Japanese consul-general in Harbin 1925–1927.

Apollonova, Klaudia (1903–1996), Sugihara's first wife.

Araki Sadao (1877–1966), army minister 1931–1934.

Arita Hachirō (1884–1965), diplomat and foreign minister 1936–1938, 1940.

Beck, Józef (1894–1944), Polish foreign minister 1932–1939.

Bielkiewicz, Anna (1877–1936), Polish resident in Vladivostok, member of Committee of Rescue 1919. Visited Japan 1920.

Beneš, Edvard (1884–1948), Czechoslovak foreign minister 1918–1935 and president 1935–1938; 1945–1948.

Carr, E. H. (1892–1982), British historian.

Chamberlain, Neville (1869–1940), British prime minister 1937–1940.

Chiang Kai-shek (Jiang Jieshi, 1887–1975), Chinese nationalist politician, general in the National Revolutionary Army, leader of the Republic of China 1928–1975.

Daszkiewicz, Leszek, Lieutenant, alias Jan Stanislaw Perz (n.d.), member of the Polish intelligence network under Michał Rybikowski, cooperated with Sugihara in Kaunas, accompanied him to Prague, Königsberg (till August 1941).

Dovidavičius, Simonas (1960–2019), director, Sugihara House, Kaunas, Lithuania.

Ding Shiyuan (1879–1945), Manchukuo ambassador to Japan 1933–1935.

Doihara Kenji (1883–1948), head of the Mukden Special Service Group.

Drummond, Eric (1876–1951), secretary general of the League of Nations, 1920–1933.

Eden, Anthony (1897–1977), lord privy seal 1934; foreign secretary 1935–1938, 1940–1945, prime minister 1955–1957, Great Britain.

Fisher, Warren, Sir (1879–1948), permanent secretary to the Treasury, Great Britain, 1919–1939.

Fujimura Michio (1929–1999), professor of Japanese political and diplomatic history, Sophia University.

Fukushima Yasumasa (1852–1919), military attaché at the Japanese legation in Berlin ca 1890.

Ganor, Solly (1928–), Lithuanian Jew.

Göring, Hermann (1893–1946), German air traffic minister 1933.

Gotō Yasutsugu (1898–?), non-career diplomat, posted to Odessa 1925, Poland 1937.

Hanaya Tadashi (1894–1957), head of the Mukden Special Service Group.

Hanihara Masanao (1876–1934), diplomat, consul-general San Francisco 1916–1918, vice-foreign minister 1919, ambassador to Washington 1922–1924.

Hara Takashi/Kei (1856–1921), prime minster 1918–1921, assassinated.

Harada Kumao (1888–1946), secretary to Saionji Kinmochi.

Hashimoto Kingorō (1890–1957), colonel in the army, involved in coup attempts in 1931.

Hayashi Senjūrō (1876–1943), army general, commander in chief Korean army, prime minister 1937.

Hirohito, Emperor (1901–1989), the 124th emperor of Japan.

Hirota Kōki (1878–1948), career diplomat, ambassador to the Soviet Union 1930–1932, foreign minister 1933–1936, prime minister 1937–1938, executed as a war criminal.

Honda Ryūhei (1896–?), diplomat, 1922. Moscow 1932, Manchuria and in Soviet territory in the Far East 1934–1939, first-class interpreter at the embassy in Moscow 1939.

Horinouchi Kensuke (1886–1979), vice-minister of the Foreign Ministry April 1936. Later ambassador to the United States 1938–1940.

Hyakutake Haruyoshi (1888–1947), head of the Harbin Special Service Group.

Hyōdō Nagao (1936–2017), ambassador in Poland 1993–1997.

Ichige Kōzō (1884–1945), consul-general, Prague 1939.

Ichikawa Hikotarō (1896–1946), diplomat, posted to Stockholm 1933 and Helsinki 1935. Author of *Bunka to gaikō* (Culture and diplomacy) 1939.

Inukai Tsuyoshi (1855–1932), prime minister (Seiyūkai) 1931–1932, assassinated.

Ishiwara/Ishihara Kanji (1889–1949), Kwantung Army 1928, triggered Manchurian Incident 1931.

Itagaki Seishirō (1885–1948), senior staff officer and chief of intelligence in the Kwantung Army, army minister 1938–1939.

Itō Nobumi (1885–1960), deputy director of the Imperial Japanese Bureau for the League of Nations, minister in Warsaw 1933–1937.

Jakubianiec, Alfons, Captain, alias Jerzy Kuncewicz ("Kuba") (n.d.) Polish intelligence agent.

Kanaya Hanzō (1873–1933), chief of the General Staff 1931.

Kanō Jigorō (1860–1938), founder of judo.

Karakhan, Lev (1889–1937), Deputy People's Commissar for Foreign Affairs, U.S.S.R.

Kase Shun'ichi (1897–1956), diplomat.

Kasai Tadakazu (n.d.), diplomat, friend of Sugihara, counselor, Japanese embassy in Germany.

Katayama Junnosuke (1914–2000), studied at Harbin Gakuin. Clerk (*shokisei*) at legation in Latvia 1936–1939, studying Russian. Passed elite diplomatic exam 1943, stationed in Egypt and Yugoslavia. Later ambassador to Liberia 1973–1977.

Katō Takaaki (1860–1926), ambassador to Great Britain 1900. Later foreign minister 1906, prime minister 1924–1926.

Kawai Hiroyuki (1883–1933), entered diplomatic service 1908, served in Paris, Petrograd, Stockholm, Brussels, and with the Peace Commission in Paris. Appointed minister to Warsaw September 1931–1933.

Kennan, George F. (1904–2005), American diplomat and specialist in Soviet affairs.

Kikuchi Setsuko (d. 1948), younger sister of Sugihara [Kikuchi] Yukiko, sister-in-law of Sugihara Chiune.

Kobayashi Takiji (1903–1933), author and communist.

Konoe Fumimaro (1891–1945), politician, prime minister 1937–1939, 1940–1941.

Kozlovsky, Benedict Ignatiev (1899–?), Soviet vice-consul Harbin 1924–27; consul-general in Shanghai, 1927; Far Eastern Bureau of the Foreign Commissariat (Narkmindel) 1927; Japan specialist, leading role in fishery negotiations 1933–1935. Visited Japan as member of delegation for CER negotiations. Head of Second Eastern Dept by 1937.

Kurihara Ken (1911–2005), scholar of Japanese diplomatic history.

Kurusu Saburō (1886–1954), diplomat, director-general of Bureau of Commercial Affairs 1932; ambassador Belgium 1936–1939, ambassador to Germany 1939–1941. Signatory of the Tripartite Pact, September 1941.

Litvinov, Maxim (1876–1951), Soviet People's Commissar for Foreign Affairs, 1930.

Maisky, Ivan (1884–1975), diplomat, Soviet ambassador to London 1932–1943.

Makino Nobuaki (1861–1949), diplomat, politician, lord keeper of the Privy Seal. Father in law of Yoshida Shigeru.

Masaryk, Tomáš (1850–1937), president of Czechoslovakia 1918–1935.

Matsudaira Tsuneo (1877–1949), diplomat, ambassador to London 1929–1935.

Matsuoka Yōsuke (1880–1946), diplomat, minister of foreign affairs 1940–1941.

Melamed, Leo (1932–), American attorney and authority on futures markets.

Merkys, Antanas (1887–1955), prime minister of Lithuania 1939–1940.

Minami Jirō (1874–1955), army minister 1931.

Miyazaki Katsutarō (1892–1946), worked in embassies in London, France (counselor), Turkey 1936, minister to Romania 1940 (resigned).

Molotov, Vyacheslav (1890–1986), Soviet politician, diplomat.

Morishima Morito (1896–1975), consul in Mukden, minister to Portugal 1942–1946.

Munters, Vilhelms (1898–1967), Latvian foreign minister 1936–1940.

Nagai Matsuzō (1877–1957), ambassador to Germany 1933–1934.

Natkevičius, Ladas (1893–1945), Lithuanian lawyer, diplomat, politician. Envoy to Moscow 1940.

Nei Saburō (1902–1992), the acting consul-general in Vladivostok 1941.

Neurath, Konstantin von (1873–1956), German foreign minister 1932–1938.

Nicholas II, Tsar (1868–1918), the last Romanov monarch.

Nishi Haruhiko (1893–1986), vice-foreign minister under Tōgō Shigenori.

Nitobe Inazō (1862–1933), academic and writer, under secretary general to the League of Nations 1920–1927.

Nomura Kichisaburō (1877–1964), admiral, foreign minster 1939–1940.

Ōhashi Chūichi (1893–1975), Japanese consul-general in Harbin 1931–1932.

Okamoto Kiyotomi, General (1894–1945), head of military mission to Germany and Italy, 1943–1944.

Onodera Makoto (1897–1987), military attaché to the Latvian legation 1936.

Onouchi Hiroshi (1899–1984), colonel in the army, Japanese military attaché in Riga 1939–1940.

Ōshima Hiroshi (1886–1975), lieutant general and vice admiral, ambassador to Berlin, 1938–1939, 1941–1945.

Ōta Hideo (1896–?), non career diplomat, entered Foreign Ministry 1922, posted in various places in the Soviet Union and the Far East, including Nikolayevsk and Harbin (1926–1929), Moscow, and Novosibirsk (vice-consul) before being appointed third secretary at Latvian legation in 1939.

Ōta Tamekichi (1880–1956), Japanese ambassador to the U.S.S.R. 1932–1936.

Ōtaka Shōjirō (1892–1966), Japanese minister to Latvia, Estonia and Lithuania 1938–1940.

Ribbentrop, Joachim von (1893–1946), German foreign minister 1938–1945.

Romer, Andrzej Tadeusz (1894–1978), Polish diplomat, ambassador to Italy, Portugal, Japan 1937–1941, minister of foreign affairs, Polish Government-in-Exile, 1943–1944.

Roosevelt, Franklin D. (1882–1945), president of the USA 1933–1945.

Rybikowski, Michał, Major, alias Peter [Piotr] Iwanow (1900–1991), Polish intelligence officer.

Saarsen, Villem (1891–1982), Estonian military attaché in Riga.

Saionji Kinmochi (1849–1940), twice prime minister and the elder statesman (genrō) with the power to nominate prime ministers.

Saitō Makoto (1858–1936), prime minister 1932–1934, assassinated in the February 26 Incident of 1936.

Sakō Shūichi (1887–1949), counselor, Japanese embassy in Moscow 1925; envoy in Helsinki 1937; ambassador to Warsaw, 1937–1939.

Sakuma Shin (1893–1987), head of the Foreign Ministry's Telegraphic Section 1934, *chargé d'affaires* Latvia 1935; first minister to Estonia, Latvia and Lithuania 1937–1938, envoy to Nazi Germany 1941.

Satō Naotake (1882–1971), foreign minister March–June 1937; ambassador to Moscow 1942–1945.

Selter, Karl (1898–1958), Estonian foreign minister 1938–1939.

Shichida Motoharu (1896–1958), *chargé d'affaires ad interim* Germany January–November 1932. First secretary in the Japanese embassy in Moscow who helped Sakō Shūichi with Sugihara's visa problem and who was later consul-general in Vladivostok and then counselor in the Moscow embassy. Minister in Afghanistan 1942–1946.

Shidehara Kijūrō (1872–1951), foreign minister 1924–1927, 1929–1931, prime minister 1945–1946.

Shigemitsu Mamoru (1887–1957), diplomat and politician, vice-foreign minister 1933, ambassador to the Soviet Union and the United Kingdom.

Shimada Shigeru (1885–1954), non career diplomat, posted to Russia/Soviet Union, Latvia 1939.

Shimura Giichi (1899–?), diplomat, intelligence agent, friend from the Harbin period.

Shiratori Toshio (1887–1949), minister to Sweden 1933–1936, ambassador to Italy 1938–1939.

Simon, John, Sir (1873–1954), British politician. Home secretary, foreign secretary, chancellor of the Exchequer.

Slavutsky, Mikhail Mikhailovich (n.d.), Soviet consul-general in Harbin 1933, ambassador to Japan 1937–1938.

Smetona, Antanas (1874–1944), president of Lithuania 1926–1940.

Stoessinger, John (1927–2017), American academic, author.

Stomonyakov, Boris (1882–1940/41), Second Deputy Commissar of Foreign Affairs 1934–1938.

Sugihara Chiune (1900–1986), diplomat.

Sugihara Yukiko (1913–2008), née Kikuchi, wife of Chiune.

Sugimura Yōtarō (1884–1939), diplomat. Under secretary general to the League of Nations 1927–1933, ambassador to Italy 1934–1937, France 1937–1938.

Sugishita Yūjirō (1893–1983), with diplomatic experience in the Japanese embassy both in the time of Imperial Russia and that of the Soviet Union. *Chargé d'affaires* in Riga 1929. *Chargé d'affaires ad interim*, Germany, October–December 1934. Minister at legation in Finland 1938–1940.

Suzuki Teiichi (1888–1989), head of Army Ministry's Newspaper Group 1933.

Tachi Sakutarō (1874–1943), emeritus professor of law at the Imperial University of Tokyo.

Tanaka Giichi (1864–1929), army minister 1918–1921, army general 1921, army minister and general 1923–1924, prime minister and foreign minister 1927–1929.

Tani Masayuki (1889–1962), diplomat, head of the Asian Bureau in the Foreign Ministry.

Tatekawa Yoshitsugu (1880–1945), ambassador to Moscow 1940–1942.

Terasaki Hidenari (1900–1951), diplomat.

Tōgō Shigenori (1882–1950), diplomat, foreign minister 1941–1942 and 1945.

Tomita Tomohiko (1920–2003), former head of the Imperial Household Agency 1978–1988.

Uchida Yasuya (1865–1936), foreign minister 1911–1912, 1918–1924 and 1932–1933, former president of SMR.

Ugaki Kazushige (1868–1956), army minister in Kenseikai/Minseitō cabinets in 1924–1927 and 1929–1931, governor-general of Korea.

Ulmanis, Kārlis (1877–1942), president of Latvia 1934–1940.

Urbšys, Juozas (1896–1991), Lithuanian diplomat, foreign minister 1938–1940.

Wakatsuki Reijirō (1866–1949), prime minister, Kenseikai/Minseitō 1926–1927 and 1931.

Wang Jingwei (1883–1944), head of the Japan-backed Reorganized National Government in Nanjing.

Warhaftig, Zorah (also Zerach), (1906–2002), lawyer from Warsaw, minister of religions, Israel 1961–1974.

Watanabe Rie (1875–?), *chargé d'affaires ad interim* in Poland and consul-general in Vladivostok.

Xie Jieshi (1878–1954), took part in negotiations between the warlord of Kirin Province and the Japanese army after the Manchurian Incident, first minister of Foreign Affairs in the Manchukuo government.

Yagi Masao (1913–2007), entered Foreign Ministry 1936, served in army 1937–1940, and, minister Taipei 1957. Consul-general San Francisco 1960–1961, ambassador to Iraq 1961–1964, ambassador to Hungary 1967–1968, ambassador to Indonesia 1969–1972.

Yagi Motohachi (1883–1946), Japanese consul-general in Harbin 1928–1931.

Yamamoto Gonbee/Gonbei (1852–1933), admiral, prime minister 1913–1914.

Yamauchi Shirō (1880–?), Japanese consul-general in Harbin 1921–1925.

Yamawaki Masataka (1886–1974), army staff officer, military attaché legation in Poland 1934–1935.

Yamaza Enjirō (1866–1914), counselor at the Japanese embassy in Great Britain, 1908–1911.

Yanagawa Heisuke (1879–1945), vice-minister of war 1932–1934.

Yasue Norihiro (1888–1950), colonel, director of the Dalian Special Service Group, 1939–1940; Jewish expert in army.

Yosano Kaoru (1938–2017), politician.

Yosano Shigeru (1904–1971), diplomat.

Yoshida Shigeru (1878–1967), diplomat, ambassador to London 1936–1938, prime minister 1946–1947 and 1948–1954.

Yoshizawa Kenkichi (1874–1965), ambassador to France, official representative to the League of Nations, foreign minister January to May 1932. Son-in-law of Inukai Tsuyoshi.

Yurenev, Konstantin (1888–1938), Soviet ambassador to Tokyo 1933–1937.

Zhang Zuolin (Chang Tso-lun, 1875–1928), Chinese warlord, Manchuria, based at Fengtian (Mukden), occupied Beijing 1926–1928.

Zwartendijk, Jan (1896–1976), businessman, honorary Dutch consul in Kaunas, issuer of "Curaçao" visas.

Bibliography

Diplomatic Archives of the Ministry of Foreign Affairs Japan

1. Meiji and Taisho eras (1868–1926)

Miscellaneous collection of documents relating to diplomatic relations between the [Japanese] empire and other foreign countries: Japanese-Polish relations, 1.1.4.1-14.

Miscellaneous matters related to secessions and mergers of various countries, 1.4.3.4 (Vol. 4).

Miscellaneous matters related to students sent abroad, Asia, reports of examination results, 6.1.7.6-3-1 (Vol. 1).

2. Showa era, early (1926–1945)

Japan-Poland relations, A.1.3.0.13.

Japan-Britain diplomatic relations (Matsumoto records), A.1.3.4.1.

General reports concerning political conditions in Europe and America, A.2.0.0.X10 (6 vols.).

Great Britain, diplomatic relations with the Soviet Union, A.2.2.0.B/R1.

Germany, diplomatic relations with Poland (including the Corridor issue), A.2.2.0.G/PO1.

Germany, diplomatic relations with the Soviet Union, A.2.2.0.G/R1.

Poland, diplomatic relations with the Soviet Union, A.2.2.0.PO/R1.

Border disputes between Poland and Lithuania, A.4.6.1.LI/PO1.

Russia (Soviet Union), domestic administration in the country, political movements of White Russians, A.6.5.0.1-2 (Vols. 3, 4).

Second European War, A.7.0.0.8.

Second European War, Germany-Poland War and Soviet occupation of Poland, A.7.0.0.8-1.

Second European War, Outbreak of Germany-Soviet War, A.7.0.0.8-37.

Greater Far Eastern War, incoming telegrams with director's code, A.7.0.0.9-63 (Vols. 1–3).

Japan-Russia Neutrality Pact (including preservation of the territory of Manchukuo and Outer Mongolia, also declaration of nonaggression), B.1.0.0.J/R1 (Vols. 1, 4).

Tripartite Pact, B.1.0.0.J/X2.

Tripartite Pact, records of discussions on German-Japanese relations centering on the Anti-Comintern Pact, B.1.0.0.J/X2-6.

German-Soviet Nonaggression Pact, B.1.0.0.G/R2.

International Cooperation (Nonaggression) Pacts in Europe, B.1.0.0.X8 (4 vols.).

Negotiations over signing of Mutual Assistance Treaties in Northeastern Europe (1934), B.1.0.0.X10.

League of Nations, entry and withdrawal, expulsion, Soviet Union, B.9.1.0.9-1.

Ethnic and national problems, Jewish problem, I.4.6.0.1-2 (13 vols.).

Foreign laws and regulations concerning passports and visas, incidents and related dealings: Soviet Union, Concerning Foreign Ministry personnel, J.2.1.0.X1-R1-1.

Reports from Diplomatic Offices Abroad Regarding Foreigners' Passports and Visas. Europe, J.2.3.0.J/X2-6 (Vol. 2).

Withdrawal of Imperial Japanese representatives from the three Baltic states upon Soviet annexation (including withdrawal of representatives of the Baltic states [from Japan] as well as of those in Manchuria), M.2.1. 0.60.

Ministry telegraphic communications, administrative, Ciphers, Incidents concerning ciphers, N.1.5. 0.1-1-9.

3. Reports

Europe and America Bureau, report 55, "General survey of the national economy of the Soviet Union," Europe 55.

Research Department, report 192, "Diplomacy with the three Baltic states," Survey 117.

Research Department, First Section, report 6, "The Soviet annexation of the three Baltic states," Survey 1-6.

4. Disclosed document of historical value

Past Errors in Japanese Diplomacy, A'.1.1.0.1.

Collections of Historical Sources

Foreign Ministry of Japan. *Nihon gaikō bunsho, Shōwa-ki II dainibu* [Documents on Japanese foreign policy, Showa period II-2] Vols. 1–5 (1996–2007).

———. *Nihon gaikō bunsho, Nichi-Doku-I sangoku dōmei kankei chōshoshū* [Documents on Japanese foreign policy, reports related to the conclusion of the Tripartite Pact] (2004).

Tsunoda Jun (ed). *Gendaishi shiryō 10: Nitchū sensō 3* [Documents on contemporary history 10: Sino-Japanese War 3]. Tokyo: Misuzu Shobo, 1964.

Memoirs

Adamkus, Valdas. *Likimo vardas: Lietuva: apie laiką, įvykius, žmones* [My fate, Lithuania: Time, events, people]. Kaunas: Santara, 1998.

Daskiewicz, L. *Placówka wywiadowcza "G". Sprawozdania i dokumenta* [Intelligence Outpost G, Reports and Documents]. London, 1948. Typescript (Romer Archive, National Library, Warsaw).

Ganor, Solly. *Light One Candle: A Survivor's Tale from Lithuania to Jerusalem.* New York: Kodansha America Inc., 1995.

Furusaki Hiroshi. *Suigin to sensō* [Mercury and war]. Kinto, 1971 (privately published).

Harada Kumao. *Fragile Victory: Prince Saionji and the 1930 London Treaty Issue from the Memoirs of Baron Harada Kumao.* Trans. with an Introduction and Annotations by Thomas Francis Mayer-Oakes. Detroit: Wayne State University Press, 1968.

Kennan, George F. *Memoirs, 1950–1963.* Boston: Little, Brown and Company, 1967.

Morishima Morito. *Inbō, ansatsu, guntō: Ichi gaikōkan no kaisō* [Plots, assassinations, swords: Memoirs of a Diplomat]. Tokyo: Iwanami Shoten, 1950.

Nishi Haruhiko. *Kaisō no Nihon gaikō* [Reminiscences of Japanese diplomacy]. Tokyo: Iwanami Shoten, 1965.

Ōhashi Chūichi. *Taiheiyō sensō yuraiki: Matsuoka gaikō no shinsō* [The origins of the Pacific War: The truth about Matsuoka Diplomacy]. Tokyo: Kaname Shobo, 1952.

Onodera Yuriko. *Barutokai no hotori nite: Bukan no tsuma no Daitōa sensō* [On the shores of the Baltic: The Greater East Asia War of a military attaché's wife]. Tokyo: K.K. Kyodo News, 1985.

Shigemitsu Mamoru. *Shigemitsu Mamoru: Gaikō kaisōroku* [Shigemitsu Mamoru: Memoirs of a diplomat]. Tokyo: The Mainichi Newspapers, 1978.

———. *Japan and Her Destiny: My Struggle for Peace.* Ed. F.S.G. Piggott. Trans. Oswald White. London: Hutchinson, 1958.

Stoessinger, John. *From Holocaust to Harvard: A Story of Escape, Forgiveness, and Freedom.* New York: Skyhorse Publishing Inc, 2014.

Sugihara Chiune. "Ketsudan: Gaikōkan no kaisō" [A decision: Memoirs of a diplomat]. Included in Watanabe Katsumasa, *Ketsudan: Inochi no biza* [A decision: Visas to save lives]. Tokyo: Taisho Shuppan, 1996.

Sugihara Yukiko. *Shinpan rokusennin no inochi no biza* [Visas for life for six thousand, new edition]. Tokyo: Taisho Shuppan, 1993.

———. *Visas for Life.* San Francisco: Edu-Comm Plus, 1995.

Uršys, Juozas. *Lietuva lemtingaisiais 1939–1940 metais* [Lithuania during the fatal years, 1939–40]. Vilnius: Mintis, 1988.

Warhaftig, Zerach. *Refugee and Survivor: Rescue Efforts During the Holocaust.* Jerusalem: Yad Vashem, 1988.

Zable, Arnold. *Café Scheherazade.* Melbourne: Text Publishing Company, 2003.

Secondary Sources

Altman, Ilya. "The Issuance of Visas to War Refugees by Chiune Sugihara as Reflected in the Documents of the Russian Archives." *Deeds and Days* (VDU Lithuania) 67 (2017): 231–237.

Brooks, Barbara J. *Japan's Imperial Diplomacy: Consuls, Treaty Ports, and War in China, 1895–1938.* Honolulu: University of Hawaii Press, 2000.

Chunichi Shimbun Shakaibu, ed. *Jiyū e no tōsō: Sugihara biza to Yudayajin* [Escape to freedom: Sugihara Visas and the Jews]. Tokyo: Tokyo Shimbun Shuppankyoku, 1995.

Coox, Alvon D. "Japanese Foreknowledge of the Soviet-German War, 1941." *Soviet Studies* 23:4 (1972): 554–572.

———. *Nomonhan, Japan against Russia 1939.* 2 vols. Stanford: Stanford University Press, 1985.

Degras, Jane, ed. *Soviet Documents on Foreign Policy. Vol. III 1933–1941.* London: Oxford University Press, 1953.

Dull, Paul S. "The Assassination of Chang Tso-lin." *The Far Eastern Quarterly* 11:4 (1952): 453–463.

Duus, Peter, Ramon H. Myers and Mark R. Peattie, eds. *The Japanese Informal Empire in China, 1895–1937.* Princeton, New Jersey: Princeton University Press, 1991.

Hall, Simon. *Blinded by the Rising Sun: Japanese Military Intelligence from the First Sino-Japanese War to the End of World War II.* Thesis submitted for the degree of Doctor of Philosophy in School of Social Sciences, University of Adelaide, 2017.

Inaba Chiharu. "Japanese Intelligence Operations in Scandinavia during World War II." *Scandinavian Journal of History* 33:2 (2008): 122–138.

———. "Documents Related to 'Visas for Life' and Historiography of Chiune Sugihara." *Deeds and Days* (VDU Lithuania) 67 (2017): 263–271.

Itō Takayuki, Inouchi Toshio and Nakai Kazuo, eds. *Shinpan sekai kakkokushi 20, Pōrando, Ukuraina, Baruto* [New world history series 20: Poland, Ukraine and the Baltic States]. Tokyo: Yamakawa Shuppansha, 1998.

Jufuku Shigeru. *Sugihara Chiune to inochi no biza: Shiberia o koete* [Sugihara Chiune and visas for life: Crossing Siberia]. Hikone: Sunrise Shuppan, 2007.

Kasekamp, Andres. *A History of the Baltic States.* Basingstoke/New York: Palgrave Macmillan, 2010.

Krebs, Gerhard. "Germany and Sugihara Chiune: Japanese-Polish Intelligence Cooperation and Counter-Intelligence." *Deeds and Days* (VDU Lithuania) 67 (2017): 215–230.

———. "The 'Jewish Problem' in Japanese-German Relations, 1933–1945." In *Japan in the Fascist Era*, ed. E. Bruce Reynolds, 107–132. New York: Palgrave Macmillan 2004.

Kudō Akira and Tajima Nobuo, eds. *Nichi-Doku kankeishi 1890–1945*. [A history of Japanese-German relations 1890–1945]. Vols 1–3. Tokyo: University of Tokyo Press, 2008.

Kudō Akira, Tajima Nobuo and Erich Pauer, eds. *Japan and Germany: Two Latecomers to the World Stage, 1890–1945*. Folkestone: Global Oriental, 2009.

Lu, David J. *Agony of Choice: Matsuoka Yōsuke and the Rise and Fall of the Japanese Empire, 1880–1946*. Lanham: Lexington Books, 2002.

Maruyama Naoki. *Taiheiyō sensō to Shanhai no Yudaya nanmin* [The Pacific War and Jewish refugees in Shanghai]. Tokyo: Hosei University Press, 2005.

———. "Facing a Dilemma: Japan's Jewish Policy in the Late 1930s." In *War and Militarism in Modern Japan*, ed. Guy Podler, 22–38. Folkestone: Global Oriental, 2009.

Masunaga Shingo. "The Interwar Japanese Intelligence Activities in the Baltic States: 1918–1940." *Acta Historica Tallinnensia* 24 (2018): 78–98.

———. "Facts Clarified? The Interwar Estonian-German-Japanese Intelligence Cooperation." *Acta Historica Tallinnensia* 25 (2019): 90–105.

Matsusaka, Yoshihisa Tak. *The Making of Japanese Manchuria, 1904–1932*. Cambridge: Harvard University Press, 2001.

Medzini, Meron. *Under the Shadow of the Rising Sun: Japan and the Jews during the Holocaust Era*. Boston: Academic Studies Press, 2016.

Miwa Kimitada. *Matsuoka Yōsuke: Sono ningen to gaikō* [Matsuoka Yōsuke: His person and diplomacy]. Tokyo: Chuo Koronsha, 1971.

Miyake Masaki. *Sutārin, Hitorā to Nisso-Doku-I rengō kōsō* [Stalin, Hitler and the concept of a coalition of Japan, the Soviet Union, Germany and Italy]. Tokyo: Asahi Shimbun Publications, 2007.

———. "The Tripartite Pact and the Idea of a Eurasian Continental Bloc." National Institute for Defense Studies (NIDS), International Forum on War History 2010: 15–47.

Murase Shinya. "Thomas Baty in Japan: Seeing through the Twilight." *The British Year Book of International Law* 73: 1 (2002): 315–342.

Nakar, Eldad. "Sugihara Chiune and the Visas to Save Lives: Assessing the Efforts to Memorialize a Japanese Hero." *Japan Focus* 6:1 (2008) https://apjjf.org/-Eldad-Nakar/2640/article.html.

Nish, Ian. "Japanese Military Intelligence on the Eve of the Manchurian Crisis." In *Collected Writings of Ian Nish, Part 2, Japan, Russia and East Asia*, 251–256. Tokyo: Edition Synapse, 2001.

———. "Nishi Haruhiko (1893–1986). Conscientious and Patriotic Bureaucrat London, 1955–57." In *Japanese Envoys in Britain 1862–1964*, 217–226. Folkestone, Global Oriental, 2007.

Nishi Haruhiko. *Kaisō no Nihon gaikō* [Reminiscences of Japanese Diplomacy]. Tokyo: Iwanami shoten, 1965.

Ōnaka Makoto. "The Relationship between Japan and the Baltic States during the Interwar Period." *Journal of Baltic Studies* 36: 4 (2005): 408–422.

Pałasz-Rutkowska, Ewa. "Major Fukushima Yasumasa and his Influence on the Japanese Perception of Poland at the Turn of the Century." In *The Japanese and Europe: Images and Perceptions*, ed. Bert Edström, 125–133. Richmond Surrey: Japan Library, 2000.

———. "The Polish Ambassador Tadeusz Romer: A Rescuer of Refugees in Tokyo." *Deeds and Days* (VDU Lithuania) 67 (2017): 239–254.

Pałasz-Rutkowska, Ewa and Andrzej, T. Romer. "Polish-Japanese Co-operation during World War II". Japan Forum, 7:2 (1995): 285–316.

———. *Historia stosunków polsko-japońskich 1904–1945* [History of Polish-Japanese relations 1904–1945]. Warsaw: Bellona, 1996; 2nd enlarged and revised edition, Warsaw: Trio, 2009; 3rd edition, Warsaw: Wydawnictwo Japonica 2019.

Plakens, Andrejs. *A Concise History of the Baltic States.* Cambridge: Cambridge University Press, 2011.

Report of the Select Committee to Investigate Communist Aggression and the Forced Incorporation of the Baltic States into the U.S.S.R. Washington, D.C.: Government Printing Office, 1954.

Shima Sonoko. *Monogatari: Baruto sangoku no rekishi* [The story of the history of the three Baltic states]. Tokyo: Chuo Koronshinsha, 2004.

Shiraishi Masaaki. *Chōhō no tensai Sugihara Chiune* [Sugihara Chiune, genius of intelligence]. Tokyo: Shinchosha, 2011.

———. *Sensō to chōhō gaikō: Sugihara Chiune tachi no jidai* [War and intelligence diplomacy: The times of Sugihara Chiune and his superiors]. Tokyo: Kadokawa, 2015.

Stoessinger, John G. *Why Nations Go to War.* Boston: Wadsworth, 2010.

Strelcovas, Simonas. "Refugees between Myth and Reality." *Deeds and Days* (VDU Lithuania) 67 (2017): 139–150.

Sugimura Yōichi, ed. *Sugimura Yōtarō no tsuioku* [Reminiscences of Sugimura Yōtarō]. Privately published, 1940.

Suzuki Tōru. *Baruto sangokushi* [History of the Baltic states]. Kanagawa: Tokai University Press, 2000.

Tajima Nobuo. *Nachizumu kyokutō senryaku: Nichi-Doku bōkyō kyōtei o meguru chōhōsen* [The Nazi Far Eastern Strategy: The intelligence war surrounding the Japanese-German Anti-Comintern Pact]. Tokyo: Kodansha, 1997.

———. "The Berlin-Tokyo Axis Reconsidered: From the Anti-Comintern Pact to the Plot to Assassinate Stalin." In *Japanese-German Relations 1895–1945. War, Diplomacy and Public Opinion*, eds. Christian W. Spang and Rolf-Harold Wippich, 161–179. London and New York: Routledge, 2006.

———. "Tripartite Pact between Japan, Germany and Italy." National Institute for Defense Studies (NIDS), International Forum on War History 2016: 45–60.

Teshima Ryūichi. *Sugihara darā* [Sugihara dollar]. Tokyo: Shinchosha, 2010.

Thorne, Christopher. *The Limits of Foreign Policy: The West, the League and the Far Eastern Crisis of 1931–1933.* London: Macmillan, 1973.

Tōmatsu Haruo and H. P. Willmott. *A Gathering Darkness: The Coming of War to the Far East and the Pacific, 1921–1942.* Lanham: SR Books, 2004.

Watanabe Katsumasa. *Ketsudan: Inochi no biza* [A decision: Visas to save lives]. Tokyo: Taisho Shuppan, 1996.

———. *Shinsō: Sugihara biza* [The truth: Sugihara Visas]. Tokyo: Taisho Shuppan, 2000.

———. *Sugihara Chiune no higeki: Kuremurin bunsho wa kataru* [The tragedy of Sugihara Chiune: Through the Kremlin archives]. Tokyo: Taisho Shuppan, 2006.

Yamaguchi Noboru. "An Unexpected Encounter with Hybrid Warfare: The Japanese Experience in North China, 1937–1945." In *Hybrid Warfare, Fighting Complex Opponents from the Ancient World to the Present*, eds. Williamson Murray and Peter R. Mansoor, 225–253. New York: Cambridge University Press, 2012.

Yasue Hiroo. *Dairen tokumu kikan to maboroshi no Yudaya kokka* [The Dairen Special Service Group and the phantom Jewish state]. Tokyo: Yahata Shoten, 1989.

Index

About the Author

Shiraishi Masaaki was born in Tokyo in 1963, he earned a master's degree in history from the Graduate School of Humanities, Sophia University. He has worked for the Diplomatic Archives of the Ministry of Foreign Affairs since 1989, beginning while still a graduate student. He specializes in Japanese diplomatic history and intelligence systems, with a particular focus on Sugihara Chiune, whom he has been researching for more than thirty years.

His published books in Japanese include *Puchāchin: Nihonjin ga ichiban suki na Roshiajin* (Putyatin: Japan's favorite Russian), *Rokusennin no inochi o sukue! Gaikōkan Sugihara Chiune* (Save six thousand lives! The diplomat Sugihara Chiune) and *Sensō to chōhō gaikō: Sugihara Chiune tachi no jidai* (War and intelligence diplomacy: The times of Sugihara Chiune and his superiors).

（英文版）杉原千畝　情報に賭けた外交官
Sugihara Chiune: The Duty and Humanity of an Intelligence Officer

2021年3月27日　第1刷発行

著　者　　白石仁章
訳　者　　関守ゲイノー
発行所　　一般財団法人出版文化産業振興財団
　　　　　〒101-0051 東京都千代田区神田神保町2-2-30
　　　　　電話　03-5211-7283
　　　　　ホームページ　https://www.jpic.or.jp/

印刷・製本所　　大日本印刷株式会社